الرحيم

محمد على صديقى
محمد حارث صديقى
وسيم الدين صديقى
شاهانه وسيم صديقى

MAKERS
of the
MUSLIM
WORLD

Abu Nuwas

"*Philip Kennedy has written a very good book on the
great (in my view greatest) Arabic poet,
Abu Nuwas ...The literary analysis is generally excellent,
balanced and erudite.*"

MAKERS
of the
MUSLIM
WORLD

Abu Nuwas
A Genius of Poetry

PHILIP F. KENNEDY

ONEWORLD
OXFORD

First Published by
Oneworld Publications
185 Banbury Road
Oxford OX27AR
England
www.oneworld-publications.com

First South Asian Paperback Edition 2009

ISBN 10: 1-85168-510-3
ISBN 13: 978-1-85168-510-3

Typeset by Jayvee, Trivandrum, India

Printed and bound at Gopsons Papers Ltd., Noida, U.P., India

CONTENTS

Preface viii
Acknowledgments xii

1 **"DANGLING LOCKS AND BABEL EYES" –
A BIOGRAPHICAL SKETCH OF ABU NUWAS
(c. 757–814)** 1

Background and origins 1
Education 3
Love for Janan 7
The Move to Baghdad 9
The "Modern" Poet 13
Sexuality 16
Character and Temperament 19
Prison 23
Sojourn in Egypt 25
Death and Afterlife 26

2 **"LOVE, WINE, SODOMY ... AND THE LASH" -
THE LYRIC POETRY OF ABU NUWAS** 29

Erotic Poetry 29
Two Traditions of Love Poetry – A Sketch 30
A Digest of Idealized Love 32
Inching towards Frivolity and Lust 35
The Psychology of Master and Servant 37
Turning the Tables 40
Pandering (to) Satan 43
Fear of Women and Other Anxieties 47
Seduction and Rape 50
Writing (and) Letters 52
Christian Boys 54

Wine Poetry 57
Beloved Wine 59
Failed Cross-Wooing and an Orgy 61
Two Views of Time 64
"Whose are the Remnants...?" 65
Trumping the Theologian 67
Dialogue with a Jewish Taverner 68
Numinous Wine 71
Jonah Comes Out of the Whale 73

3   **"THE GOOD, THE BAD AND THE UGLY" –
ON PANEGYRIC AND SATIRE** 79

The Panegyric 79
A. Formal and Sober 82
B. Less Formal and Less Sober 89
C. Occasional and Miscellaneous Eulogy 92

"Pens Dipped in Bitter Gall" – Satire 94
Bread and Bereavement 96
The Politics of State and al-Amin 97
Spite and Sacrilege 98
Tasteless Ja'far the Barmecide 101
The Alchemist and Phony Genealogies 102
Isma'il ibn Abi Sahl 102
The Stolen Member 103
Quack Philosopher of Egypt 104
Onanist Job 104
A Prison Consultation 105
Servants and Singing Girls 105
Fatal Provocation? 106

4   **SOME HUNTING POEMS AND A GAME OF
POLO** 109
A Saluki Hound 111
The Cheetah 114

Elegy for a Hound 116
The Polo Match 117

5 **"POETRY FOR MORTALS AND THE DEAD" –
ON THE ASCETIC POEM AND
THE ELEGY** 121

The Ascetic Poem 121
A Righteous Dowry 123
Man's Mortal Genealogy 124
The Danger of Empty Talk 125
Eloquent Simplicity 125
Sound and Meaning 127
The Permanent Ink of the Angels 128

The Elegy 129
For Harun al-Rashid (d. 809) 130
For Muhammad ibn Zubayda "al-Amin" (d. 813) 130
For the Barmecides 130
Fragment for His Son 131
For Waliba ibn al-Hubab 131
For a Sick Friend 132
For Himself 133

An Afterword – "Walk the Even Path with Me ..." 135
Bibliography 139
Index 142

PREFACE

M edieval Arab society produced a fabulously, perhaps uniquely rich tradition of poetry which had an important role in defining cultural identity in pre-Islamic Arabia and the Muslim world alike. Any summary of the great poets of this tradition contains a handful of steady fixtures: usually Imru' al-Qays (*fl.* early sixth century); perhaps al-Shanfara (sixth century), Majnun Layla (seventh century), 'Umar ibn Abi Rabi'a (d. 712), Abu Tammam (d. 845), al-Mutanabbi (d. 965) ...; and always in any list, except one that is unfairly censoring, Abu Nuwas (d. *c.* 814). His talent was extraordinary and showed in the matchless range and variety of his verse. He mastered most of the genres of Arabic poetry; he had an innate dexterity with words and in the formulation of ideas; he respected the spirit of inherited convention without ever being bound by its expression or "false compare"; and he was unusually poised in his employment of developing rhetorical devices (which some of his Abbasid peers could exploit excessively).

Abu Nuwas perfected two Arabic genres: the wine poem and the hunting poem. But he is remembered mainly for the former, with its erotic (often homosexual) elements, and especially for the licentiousness associated with it. His wine poetry and erotic poetry were by any standards singularly inventive; and when we add to them the remarkable sting of his invective verse he is not unjustly compared to the Earl of Rochester whose venomous yet somehow elegant poetic duels with poets of the court of Charles II are quite the apt measure of Abu Nuwas's Arabic for the Anglophone reader. But there is more than the great Rochester in Abu Nuwas. Reading widely through his poetry one might come to sense that genius shows itself in amazingly similar ways in different cultures: there are reminiscences of Keats's wine "cool'd a long age in the deep delvèd earth" with its "beaded bubbles winking at the brim"; Ronsard's *Hymne de Bacchus*, with its alloy of pagan and monotheistic elements; Marvel's seductive *To His Coy Mistress*; the tricky fluency of Skelton who was "so much more than the brilliant eccentric for which we are apt to mistake him"; and there is the Goliardic exuberance of the *Carmina Burana* alongside the gravity of Donne's *Meditations*.

The list, along with the whole comparative exercise, becomes forced the longer it gets. It is naïve and unfair to appear exclusively to measure the achievements of one culture against those of another, though part of the delight of humanistic reading is to make connections. In fact, it is just as essential for the non-specialist to be told briefly what Arabic poetry is not. There are no extensive narrative poems. No verse dramas. Readers accustomed to, say, *The Odyssey, Divina Commedia, Canterbury Tales, Hamlet, Paradise Lost, The Prelude*, etc., may well believe that in order to be great a poet should compose poems of epic length. Yet Arabic poetry has its own largely unique norms and conventions: of form, meter, subject and the distinct collocation of themes. It can, of course, only be judged fully on these terms. The former (rhyme, form, meter, etc.) are largely trapped in the enhanced Arabic of the original poetry; but one can endeavor to translate and discuss the essential spirit of the themes. It is hoped that the latter will begin to emerge, according to distinctive genres and relating to the strong literary persona of Abu Nuwas, in the course of this introductory work.

The poems discussed in this book were all written in sustained monorhyme. They were of no fixed length, varying from fragments of two-to-five verses to poems of up to forty verses; each verse was divided into two hemistich halves (as I have tried to represent in the format of my translations). Each poem was written in one of a number of quantitative meters based on sustained patterns of long and short syllables. Some poems discussed in this book are quoted in full; however, much poetry is

excerpted and this is indicated either in the accompanying
prose commentary or by the use of ellipses ("...").

The reader may find the following brief glossary of Arabic
poetic terms useful:

Badi' the collective term for a number of rhetorical devices
   developed in the eighth century and characteristic of
   Abbasid poetry in its heyday
Ghazal love/erotic poetry
Hija' satire, satirical poetry
Khamriyya a wine poem
Madih praise poetry
Marthiya an elegy
Mu'allaqa a "suspended ode", one of seven (some say ten)
   poems considered paragons of pre-Islamic poetry;
   according to legend they were suspended on the walls of
   the Ka'ba in Mecca in recognition of their quality
Muhdath "Modern" – a term used to describe the poets
   of the mid-eighth century onwards whose style was influ-
   enced by rhetorical badi'; they are distinguished in literary
   history from the "Ancient" Bedouin poets whose language
   and style, though greatly admired, were more archaic
Mujun profane, libertine or dissolute poetry
Naqida one half of a satirical duel
Nasib the opening movement of the multi-themed qasida (it
   is associated with an amatory theme and elegiac mood, and
   influenced some developments in ghazal)
Qasida multi-themed "ode", the single most important
   poetic form from pre-Islamic to modern times
Tardiyya a hunting poem
Zuhdiyya an ascetic poem

The following abbreviations are used:

EAL The Encyclopedia of Arabic Literature
Diwan the "collected poetry" of Abu Nuwas

All references to the *Diwan* are taken from the Wagner/ Schoeler critical edition (Wagner edited vols. 1 to 3 and 5; Schoeler edited vol. 4), and are indicated, e.g., as follows: *D.* ii, 45; in rare instances Ghazali's edition has been used and therefore specified; some references are to the Saqi edition of the libertine/*mujun* poems: *al-Nusus al-Muharrama* (*The Forbidden Poems*, abbreviated to *FP* in source references).

ACKNOWLEDGMENTS

I am indebted to a number of individuals: to the anonymous reader whose extraordinary erudition revealed him to be the Laudian Professor of Arabic, Geert Jan van Gelder; to Professor Ewald Wagner for his monumental scholarship on Abu Nuwas; to Patricia Crone for her formidable editing, for her vision and remarkable energy; to Victoria Roddam for patience and a sense of urgency perfectly combined; to Judy Kearns for the forbearance of a fine copy editor; to Marianne Catalan-Kennedy for encouragement and helpful frankness about endlessly splintering drafts; to Michael Gilsenan for brokering a generous sabbatical from New York University; to Jean Andréoletti for a haven in a hoopoe's garden; and to Marie-Noëlle Cordoliani for the kind offer of a room looking out upon the Tyrrhenian sea.

Philip F. Kennedy
Aléria, June 2004

"DANGLING LOCKS AND BABEL EYES"

A Biographical Sketch of Abu Nuwas
(c. 757–814)

Background and Origins

Without a shadow of doubt one of the greatest, most versatile and celebrated of classical Arabic poets was the man known fondly during his lifetime – and ever since – by the sobriquet, or Arabic "cognomen", Abu Nuwas ("He of the Dangling Locks"), a nickname he acquired as a boy or adolescent in Basra in southern Iraq where he grew up. His full name was Abu 'Ali al-Hasan ibn Hani' al-Hakami, and while to posterity he is simply Abu Nuwas, his friends and contemporaries addressed him just as often as Abu 'Ali. He was born in the province of Ahwaz, in the region of Khuzistan (ancient Elam) in south west Persia *circa* 757 CE. Puzzlingly this varies as much as 21 years in the classical sources; but he was in any case well over fifty years of age by the time of his death in the year 814 or 815, following the death of the caliph Muhammad al-Amin, son of Harun al-Rashid (d. 809), in September 813. The consensus is that he was about 59 years of age when he died..

His Persian mother, Jullaban, was a seamstress of modest background (who may also have worked selling bamboo artifacts) and who apparently never mastered the Arabic language. Her house is said to have been a meeting place for singing girls.

She was widowed around the time of Abu Nuwas's birth, but appears at some point to have remarried, as evidenced by a line of satire directed at Abu Nuwas by one of his nemeses in his later years in Baghdad ("What is your mother doing with that 'Abbas?!"). She outlived her son and Abu Nuwas's paltry estate came into her possession upon his death. It is said he bequeathed her as little as 200 dinars – astonishingly little given his eminence as a poet and the rewards that were probably heaped upon him, sporadically, during his lifetime. Unlike his mother, Abu Nuwas both mastered and crafted the Arabic language as well as any poet ever has and it provided him with a living, but he was also recklessly generous and a hedonist to boot – he suffered materially from the very same impulse that enriched his poetry.

He probably never knew his father, Hani' ibn 'Abd al-Awwal, who had served in the army of the last Umayyad caliph, Marwan II (d. 750); Hani''s grandfather, al-Sabbah, had served Jarrah ibn 'Abdullah al-Hakami, a clan of the south Arabian tribe of Sa'd ibn 'Ashira. This ethnicity is important in that a distinct, quasi-political feature of Abu Nuwas's poetry was his at times pronounced disdain for the northern Arabian tribes. This north-south tribal dichotomy constituted in broad terms a sort of Jets-versus-Sharks enmity in Umayyad and early Abbasid political society. Medieval philologists declared pithily that there were three great poets of the "Yemen" (which stands here for the southern group): Imru' al-Qays, Hassan ibn Thabit (the "court poet" of Muhammad the Prophet) and Abu Nuwas. Significantly, while it may be that Abu Nuwas acquired his sobriquet simply on account of his disheveled appearance, another explanation is that it signals his South Arabian affili-ation due to its obvious evocation of the pre-Islamic Yemeni king Dhu Nawas.

The Persian origins of Abu Nuwas's mother, Jullaban, has been significant in discussions about the poet's cultural sympa-thies. Yet the question of whether or not Abu Nuwas was an Arab or Persian poet *at heart*, is misplaced. He doubtless considered himself overwhelmingly to be an Arab poet – one firmly set within the Arab tradition; he was simply influenced in a relatively minor key by elements of a Persian ambience, as manifested in his celebrations of Nawruz and in the use of Persian vocabulary and names that pepper some fragments of his verse. Though in early Abbasid society there was an important and vociferous pro-Persian movement of literary figures, Abu Nuwas himself was anything but consistent and probably abhorred the complacency of any trenchant cultural, theological or political view. He could, for example, make fun of Muhra, the mother of his beloved Janan, for her *métier* as a procuress and tie that to her incompetence in Arabic exhibited partly in her use of Persian words – he was caricaturing her for a kind of lewd *déformation professionelle*. In sum, he simply had a more ethnically diverse background than some of his contemporaries in the Baghdad circle of the early ninth century.

Education

In his early childhood Abu Nuwas followed his mother to Basra in lower Iraq where he attended Qur'an school. Ahwaz held little promise for a family whose breadwinner had just died, and the move to Basra was doubtless motivated by a quest for livelihood, if not fortune. It was a cultural heartland. Abu Nuwas became a Hafiz (i.e., he memorized the Qur'an) at a young age; indeed his deep knowledge of the Scripture would manifest itself consistently in the linguistic tissue of his later poetry. His youthful good looks and innate charisma attracted the attention of the Kufan poet, Abu Usama Waliba ibn al-Hubab al-Asadi (d. 170/786). The latter was a handsome blond and blue-eyed man of Persian extraction who took Abu Nuwas to Kufa as a young apprentice.

The influence upon Abu Nuwas exerted by this light-spirited and nigh-delinquent poet should not be understated; there are many lasting traces of the impact he had upon the young poet, especially in his more iconoclastic mood. Waliba's poetry is homoerotic, licentious, skilled and eloquent, yet light of diction, and it is particularly in his facetious treatment of the Devil as a topos that he clearly left his mark on Abu Nuwas, who made much of this theme in his later years as a Bacchic poet. According to one tradition the Devil (Ar. Iblis from Gk. *diabolos*) played a concrete role in the relationship between Waliba and his pupil: Iblis appeared to Waliba in a dream and said of Abu Nuwas: "I will lead astray the Community of Muhammad with this youth of yours; I will not be satisfied until I sow love for him in the hearts of all hypocrites and lovers on account of his sweet and pleasant verse."

By all accounts Waliba intuitively recognized in Abu Nuwas his talent as a poet and encouraged him toward this vocation. But it is also clear that Waliba was attracted sexually to the young Hakamite and may have had erotic relations with him. Whether or not this predisposed Abu Nuwas to visit this behavior upon others when he was older can only be mooted, but certainly Abu Nuwas's relationships with adolescent boys when he had matured as a man seem to mirror his own experience with Waliba.

On the evening of their first encounter, one tradition has it, the two men drank together and ate. When Abu Nuwas removed his clothes, Waliba beheld his corporal beauty and kissed his behind at which point the young man farted in his face. Waliba cursed him for being so vulgar but Abu Nuwas retorted confidently with a maxim: "What reward can there be for the one who kisses ass except a fart!" The exchange is rude and trifling but it is of some significance in that Abu Nuwas is so often recorded as outwitting his associates. He was willing to heed advice, though, and this is nowhere more evident than in his relationship with the other man who had a profound effect on his poetic formation: Khalaf al-Ahmar (d. 796).

Returning to Basra from Kufa still an adolescent, Abu Nuwas became a disciple of this eminent transmitter and forger of early poetry. Khalaf is connected in Arabic literary history with the fabrication of a number of early poems, including conceivably — the issue has never been settled — the superb *Lamiyyat al-'Arab* ("The L-Poem of the Arabs") attributed to al-Shanfara al-Azdi (*fl.* sixth century). While Waliba was quintessentially a poet of his time, and one of the so-called "Dissolutes of Kufa," Khalaf was a philological master of the great tradition of ancient bedouin poetry and had both the authority and innate skill to round Abu Nuwas's poetic education.

If Abu Nuwas was to become the quintessential "Modern" (Ar. *muhdath*) poet of the early Abbasid efflorescence, yet he was bred certainly from the pre-Islamic tradition which he came to refashion. In this connection, it is essential to understand the often layered textual allusions of his verse which Khalaf was at least in part responsible for nurturing. This is the basic point to be gleaned from the most famous and quasi-legendary incident in their relationship. When the young Abu Nuwas asked Khalaf for permission to compose poetry of his own (somewhat disingenuously, as he doubtless already had), he was told: "Only once you have learnt by heart a thousand ancient poems". Abu Nuwas disappeared for a while then returned, announcing that he had memorized the requisite amount. He recited them out aloud over several days and then reiterated his initial request. But Khalaf now insisted that his pupil forget all the poems which he had just learnt. After a period of seclusion in a monastery Abu Nuwas forgot the poems and was *finally* authorized to compose. The incident smacks of the imaginary in the terms that it is related and it probably simply marks the formal induction of Abu Nuwas as a poet at the hands of Khalaf. However, it also helps one to appreciate the fact that in his mature years Abu Nuwas never aped the ancient corpus; rather he would be subliminally affected by it.

The ninth-century literary critic, poet and caliph-for-one-day, Ibn al-Mu'tazz, attested with authority to Abu Nuwas's sound understanding of *fiqh* (Islamic jurisprudence), acquired young: he was conversant with fundamental legal opinions and their technicalities; some of this can be sensed in his verse. In addition to his profound knowledge of prophetic traditions

(Hadith) he was proficient in particular scriptural issues, such as the complex subject of how some Qur'anic verses can qualify or supersede (abrogate) others. He studied Qur'an recitation with Abu Muhammad Ya'qub ibn Ishaq al-Hadrami, responsible for one of the ten recognized early recitations of the Scripture; Ya'qub even declared that his pupil was the best reciter of the Qur'an in Basra, despite, we might note, the adolescent's lisp (he couldn't roll his r's) but perhaps because of his husky voice. All the above bespeaks further the thorough education he received in Basra. While Khalaf al-Ahmar must certainly have instructed him in tribal lore, it was Abu 'Ubayda Ma'mar ibn al-Muthanna (d. 824) in particular who would have filled out his knowledge of the pre-Islamic tribal "Battle Days." Abu 'Ubayda was the greatest repository of this significant corpus of knowledge in early Abbasid times and remains the principal source for the extant corpus of this literature. In the rivalry between Abu 'Ubayda and al-Asma'i, another illustrious philologist and anthologist of poetry, Abu Nuwas sided naturally with Abu 'Ubayda.

This did not prevent him ridiculing his tutor by writing graffiti on the pillar of a mosque alluding to the fact that the latter enjoyed sex with boys: "God bless Lot and his tribe [of sodomites]; say, Amen! O Abu 'Ubayda! At over seventy you are the last of them ...!" A burlesque scene survives in apocrypha of Abu 'Ubayda, bereft of all dignity, holding his catamite upon his shoulders, demanding that the writings be erased – no doubt, to the scornful mirth of those who sat and watched. The boy had trouble erasing all elements of the verse and the word "Lot" remained visible, at which Abu 'Ubayda remarked tetchily that this was the one word they were trying to "flee from" – "erase it quickly!" he insisted. But Abu 'Ubayda was neither devoid of humor nor gravity, and his opinion that Abu Nuwas was for the "Modern poets" (al-muhdathun) what Imru' al-Qays was for the Ancients carries weight. Such a judgment could surely only be made once Abu Nuwas had reached a maturity in his art; the contact between Abu 'Ubayda and Abu Nuwas must have been on some level – intellectually – a lasting one, and there was no persistent rancor between the two men.

Abu Nuwas not only studied but also taught prophetic traditions (Hadith), and among his own pupils were said to be the great polymath al-Jahiz (d. 869) and the distinguished jurist al-Shafi'i (d. 820). Two traditions are transmitted by him with chains of transmission going back to the Prophet. Al-Dhahabi (d. 1348) in his *Mizan*, and no doubt other authors, judged that Abu Nuwas was essentially unworthy of transmitting Hadith due to his dissolute and immoral character. It is certainly the case that Abu Nuwas could be contemptuous of the protocols of this religious literature in his poetry; in one 10-line piece, apparently composed in Basra, he parodied the chains of transmission that provide the very authenticity of prophetic deeds and sayings. The story goes: Abu Nuwas attended the salon in Basra of 'Abd al-Wahid ibn Ziyad to which students of Hadith thronged for instruction. Each pupil was allowed to ask three questions before departing and when Abu Nuwas's turn came he simply recited the following poem: "We have transmitted on the authority of Sa'id from 'Ubada/from Zurara ibn Baqi that Sa'd ibn 'Ubada / said: 'Whosoever screws his lover will gain happiness from him; / but if he dies of doting fondness he will gain the recompense equal to reciting the Shahada (Muslim testimony of God's unity) …'"This scurrilous poem, among other details, goes on to give prominence to Jarada, a pander of Basra whose name shares the rhyme scheme of the poem with the respected transmitters of Hadith alluded to transparently, though distorted by concoction, in the first two lines.

Love for Janan

It was during his early life in Basra that Abu Nuwas fell for the only woman he is deemed truly to have loved – Janan. She was the slave-girl of the family of al-Wahhab ibn 'Abd al-Majid al-Thaqafi, a tutor of the eminent religious scholars Ahmad ibn Hanbal and al-Shafi'i. Janan was exquisitely beautiful, intelligent and learned in Arab lore (*akhbar*) and poetry. It may be that Abu Nuwas already enjoyed a reputation as a homosexual by the time he first set eyes upon her, for it is said that he caused surprise among the companions who witnessed his enrapture at the sight of her. It has even been suggested, with only the vaguest evidence, that Janan herself was a lesbian. The relationship between the two was, in any case, complicated and characterized by oscillations between attraction and antipathy expressed in animated poetic exchanges. Abu Nuwas's poems about her circulated in Basra, according to tradition, before they ever met, and this at least supports the view that he had already enjoyed a reputation as a poet before this affair. The poet's continued rhapsodies of love met with her disdain, and when it reached him that she had cursed these indiscretions his response was: "Your curse has come to my ears. Curse then all you will. Does not my name thus pass through your lips?! What more could I ask for?" In a clever conceit he continues: "I have conjectured about you in so many different ways, for is not Knowledge of the Unseen the exclusive province of God?" Even she, the point is, cannot predict the success or failure of his courtship, since only God has knowledge of the future.

When Janan declared her solemn intention of performing the pilgrimage to Mecca, Abu Nuwas determined to accompany her. Piety apparently had no initial part to play in his performance of this rite, though it is related that once he was in Mecca, having donned the garbs of ritual purity, people flocked around him to listen to the pious verse he had composed for the occasion. More famous is the following story about this visit (told by an authority of some repute): "We made the pilgrimage the same year as Abu Nuwas, and we all gathered together to perform the circumambulation of the Ka'ba. He stepped out in front of me and I saw him following a woman round, though I didn't yet know who she was. I then progressed to the Black Stone and beheld the woman kissing the stone and there he was kissing it alongside her in such a way that their cheeks touched.

I said to myself, 'He is the most perverse of people!'Then I realized this was Janan.When they had departed, I met up with him and told him, 'You wretch! Does not even this holy site bring you to your senses!' He answered that I was a fool to think that I would have crossed so many deserts and desolate tracts for any other reason!" Abu Nuwas then recited his poem about this encounter, verses redolent of the character and antics of the philandering 'Umar ibn Abi Rabi' a century earlier; he only lightly minced words: "We did at the Mosque what the pious were *not* doing."

He was once reprimanded by a judge in Basra, who hadn't at first recognized him, for talking openly to a woman in the street.The lady in question was a messenger for Janan and when Abu Nuwas justified his encounter in verse, the judge suddenly realized with whom he was dealing and vowed never to bother him again for fear of being satirized.Yet again we sense that Abu Nuwas was already established locally during the time of this affair, but it is hard properly to gauge the nature of the actual relationship; some traditions tell us that Abu Nuwas moved to Baghdad soon after it ended with a heavy heart, others that it was he who was largely responsible for its demise having refused to accede to Janan's conditions when offered her hand by her mistress – that he give up sleeping with boys. He moved to Baghdad in 786 CE, around the time of Harun al-Rashid's accession, probably not so much heartbroken as to promote his literary vocation.There, over four decades, he spent his halcyon days as well as some of his darkest moments.

The Move to Baghdad

In Baghdad success as a poet depended essentially on patronage, and we know something of his dealings with the various "maecenic" figures of the day.At the center of this was the caliphal court, but just as important were the Barmecides and their literary entourage, and other patrons, notably the family of al-Fadl ibn al-Rabi' whom Abu Nuwas embraced (or vice versa) when acceptance into the Barmecide circle was thwarted. He expressed exasperation at the stuffiness of the atmosphere at court, where one could only speak when spoken to. Here he felt the "hot embers of impatience" and would long for his friends, his style cramped by the stately protocols of comportment. It is certainly true that his finer poems reflect antics among friends and cup-companions when released from the behavioral strictures of court life; this attitude would only change, seemingly, during the reign of the caliph al-Amin whom he attended more as companion than subject.

The Barmecide family were renowned for their generous patronage, yet the poet's initial attempts to benefit from it were unsuccessful. The poet's greatest obstacle in this respect was Aban ibn 'Abd al-Hamid al-Lahiqi (d. 815–816), a poet who controlled the purse-strings of Barmecide patronage, rewarding poets according to *his* judgment of their worth. He appears to have feared Abu Nuwas as a rival, and belittled him in particular in 795 when al-Fadl ibn Yahya al-Barmaki returned from Khurasan where he had been posted as governor; Aban stood in judgment of the eulogies composed for al-Fadl on the occasion and rewarded Abu Nuwas's poem with a meager – and insulting – two dinars. Abu Nuwas slapped Aban in the face and accused him of having stolen his own mother's earnings, intimating that she made her living as a prostitute. Al-Fadl, amused by the incident, gave instructions that Aban "patch it up" with Abu Nuwas. No such truce survives in his verse: Abu Nuwas wrote a number of satires upon Aban, suggesting in one that his mother (with whom he appears to have been fixated) had confused letters when she gave him his name: she had meant to call him Atan, which in Arabic means a donkey. Aban wrote a poem of self-praise which he had sent to al-Fadl ibn Yahya; Abu Nuwas parodied this poem stingingly, ending his riposte to it with what became a proverbial line: "What I have said about you is authentic and eternal, while your words will be blown away by the wind." Aban offered Abu Nuwas a fortune to suppress this satire, but was told simply to grin and bear the stigma.

While the tension between these two poets appears never to have abated, Abu Nuwas did preserve some contact with the Barmecides. A mournful line in praise of al-Fadl ibn Yahya suggests he still had dealings with the Barmecides shortly before their downfall ("… though you have been visibly humbled, yet I have not betrayed my love for you"). Fragments of poetry survive in which he laments their terrible debacle in 803 in which many of them died. Indeed, he took a poor view of one Isma'il ibn Sabih who took over one of their high administrative functions having served them as their secretary and, adding insult to injury, divulged some of their secrets in the process. The poet's retribution for this betrayal was to write a lewd poem about Isma'il's son Muhammad – thus satisfying two desires at once.

The success Abu Nuwas achieved with Harun al-Rashid, relatively paltry though it was, was probably due not to the Barmecide family but the intercession of the Al Nawbakht already after the fall of the former in 803 and once al-Fadl ibn al-Rabi' had become the caliph's chief minister. Some sources suggest that the caliph shut the poet out completely, but had Abu Nuwas received no recognition from al-Rashid it is unlikely that he would have elegized him upon his death in 809.

Panegyric poems were written also for al-Amin and survive from the period when the latter was still only heir to the caliphate. These poems are less formal than both the status of the patron and tenor of the genre normally required, a fact which bespeaks the friendship and bonhomie between the two men. There may even have been a more charged affection between them, as evidenced by the following, clearly amorous lines: "I am in love but cannot say with whom; I fear him who fears no one! / When I think about my love for him, I feel for my head and wonder if it is still attached to my body!" (D. iv, 195) It is assumed these verses refer to al-Amin; if they do, Abu Nuwas was probably right to be coyer in this instance than he usually was in such matters.

His staunchest patrons in Baghdad were the Nawbakht family, in particular the four sons of Abu Sahl ibn Nawbakht: 'Abdallah, al-Fadl, Sulayman and Isma'il, and the latter's own son, al-Hasan. Anecdotes survive of their friendship: they drank together and the poet was rewarded financially as well as, on one occasion, with a slave-girl bought for him by Sulayman. Given that the Nawbakht family was largely responsible for the survival of Abu Nuwas's poetry after his death, it is puzzling that only one panegyric devoted to them survives as against a number of biting satires.

The most significant contact he had in Baghdad was with a welter of poets. He had various dealings in Baghdad with most of the great bards of the day, by turns amicable and hostile. The list of these relations reads like a Who's Who of the poetic luminaries at the turn of the ninth century: al-Husayn ibn al-Dahhak (some of whose Bacchic poetry appears to have been ascribed to Abu Nuwas); Muslim ibn al-Walid; Abu al-'Atahiya, who wrote homiletic poetry chiefly and was jealously proprietorial of the genre; and al-'Abbas ibn al-Ahnaf, a courtly love lyricist and favorite of Harun al-Rashid in this respect.

Like the work of most poets Abu Nuwas's *oeuvre* was not biographical, except perhaps in a topical way. However, his migration to the Abbasid capital was marked in real terms by a *khamriyya* (or wine poem) in which the pleasures of life in Baghdad, or some outlying monastery, are set up as a consoling imaginary against the lost – "pious" – youth of his Basran days. The poem is a descriptive fantasia anchored in one central feature to the poet's biography and must have been written some time after his move: "The prayer-place is now effaced [as are my old haunts], the sand dunes of the two market places of Mirbad and Labab — /Faded is the mosque which [once] brought together noble qualities and religion, faded too are al-Sihan and al-Rahab. /Abodes where I spent my youth until greyness appeared in my side-whiskers, /Amongst young men like swords, shaken by the bloom of youth, and adorned with good manners. /Then Time brought its afflictions ... /Qatrabbul is *now* my spring residence, and in the villages around al-Karkh I spend my summer – my mother now is the grape-vine."[1] (*D.* iii, 29–31) The poem emerges further into the present in a detailed Bacchic vignette: a Christian monastic context is suggested by the relief carved on golden goblets of wine: "Vessels smooth and sleek, engraved with depictions of priests and crucifixes, / Reciting their Gospel, whilst above them lay a heaven of wine, / Like pearls, scattered about by the hands of virgins taken by a playful mood." (*D.* iii, 34–35) It is the "playful mood" that really marks this poem, and bespeaks most clearly the underlying poetic inspiration and temper. Here the archetypical move (of the ancient and traditional ode) from decadent youth to respectable and forbearing present is overturned, allowing simultaneously some *real* nostalgia for Basra to be felt. The poem may not depict Baghdad – it quite clearly doesn't – however, it is a choice product of the extended Baghdadi period of the poet's life. It is in this period that Abu Nuwas matured as a poet, and this is nowhere better glimpsed than in the complexity of his lyric verse, both bacchic and erotic, that dates in bulk from this period. The *khamriyya* which Abu Nuwas mastered and perfected as a genre in the Abbasid capital allows one to situate the man best of all as a poet, absorbing and transforming a whole tradition, and as a person more generally who, in some minimal measure at the very least, was also reacting to his environment.

The "Modern" Poet

In reviewing the wine song we must note: (i) its literary genealogy, of which Abu Nuwas was so clearly conscious (and respectful of, on the whole): he clearly saw himself as the

---

[1] Mirbad was a market and famous meeting place for poets outside Basra; Qatrabbul was a village near Baghdad renowned for its viticulture and taverns; al-Karkh was the suburb to the south west of Baghdad celebrated for its commerce – it is here that Abu Nuwas appears to have lived.

inheritor of a pre-Islamic tradition, and in particular of the poetry of al-A'sha (d. *c.* 629) whom he often alluded to and even cited (see Chapter 2) – he had, in Dryden's phrase, "the genius to improve an invention"; (ii) the realism it contains, and how it represents a material culture the poet was exposed to, for all that it is a work spun from the contrary impulses of convention and a feverish imagination; (iii) the principal characteristics which he developed in the genre – they in fact mark the evolving rhetorical contours of the period as well as any other, more conservative and canonical, texts; the intellectual conceits of his poetry, and the application of the rhetorical devices known collectively as *badi'*, made him the quintessential "Modern" (*muhdath*) poet.

Briefly, in respect of (iii), Abu Nuwas cultivated four principal aspects in the construction of his wine songs: (i) the deft coupling of erotic and Bacchic themes; (ii) two complementary, at times disjunctive, views of Time: the strictures of piety (and an awareness of eschatological salvation) being offset by, and even accommodated with, the urgency of the pagan sense of "seizing the day"; (iii) a varied rhetorical impulse, providing a powerful rationale for drinking in a culture of poetic contention and satire; (iv) the ambiguity that could be preserved within a religious society by treating the themes of repentance and contrition as emergent from, and simultaneously in competition with, pagan – and still valid – values of comportment.

All of the above can be illustrated to some extent through one paradigmatic work: a seduction poem in which the tawdry closing scene parodies the chaste overture. Wine is described in a central passage in a mythic and metaphorical delineation of its age and provenience. Whilst cast tacitly as the instrument of seduction it preserves its own numinous qualities, and all blame, if there is any blame to go round, attaches to human agency. The poem is integrally structured upon an antithesis between its beginning and end, as intimated already, which is essential since such contrast is one of the cardinal features of *badi'*. The poem is also saturated with metaphor, parallelism and paronomasia (sophisticated punning), three of the other principal features of *badi'* and Modern poetry. Excerpts of the poem:

The amorous overture

O enchanting eyes, you are forever languid,
  Your stare draws out secrets held close in the heart! ...
Consider the two of us: you have rent me to pieces, though you
  Are bare of the garment in which Fate has draped me
You work to kill me with no hope of vengeance,
  As if to kill me is ritual offering to God.

The transition to wine

[So] drink the wine, though forbidden,
  For God forgives even grave sins.
A white wine forging bubbles when mixed – pearls set in gold;
She was on the Ark in Noah's time –
  Most noble of his shipment whilst the Earth was awash ...

Consummation

Auspicious stars had risen on this night
  When drunkard assaulted drunkard
We passed the time kowtowing to the Devil,
  Until the monks sounded the bells at dawn
And [a young adolescent] left, dragging delightful robes
  Which I had stained with my iniquitous behavior,
Saying, "O woe!" as tears overcame him,
  "You have torn away the [dignity] I had preserved."
I replied, "A lion saw a gazelle and lunged at it;
  Such is the variety of Fate's vicissitudes!" (D. iii, 323–5)

In a parodic turn, inviting his audience to recognize the reversal of poetic conventions, Abu Nuwas has slain the chaste gazelle at whose hands he suffered in the opening lines. Wine intoxicates but recedes from the picture, preserving its sublime qualities – quite the contrary of the lost dignity of the youth.

Sexuality

The eroticism of this poem, in which it is a young male who is rudely seduced, summons one to pause upon the sexuality of Abu Nuwas. In his far-ranging and magisterial study of homosexuality in Islamic culture, Everett K. Rowson writes: "While scholars have often remarked that Abu Nuwas's verses on women tend to be more conventional, and less enthusiastic, than those about boys, there is considerable parallelism between the two ... we have numerous examples from Abu Nuwas's own poetry, as well as that of his contemporaries, of the convention whereby women are described, and even addressed in the masculine. And the descriptive phrases employed – slender waist, black eyes, pearly teeth, and so on – are equally applicable to both sexes. Often, however, sheer circumstance makes it clear that the referent is a boy ..." The seductive enchantment of "a stare from Babel", a place associated with magic in Islamic culture, could apply to women or men. But Abu Nuwas did express preference for men unambiguously in a number of poems in which he vowed never again to risk the dangers of the "sea", i.e. women, when he could ride and travel by "land", scilicet upon the backs of men. He composed one such poem on the occasion of his marriage. We know little about this betrothal, which appears to have been forced upon him; he felt little satisfaction at the union however, effectively lampooning his wife on the very evening of their wedding.

Young adolescent boys became his sexual preference. Rowson observes that "he could be specific about the ideal age of the beloved ... Whatever the boy's age ... the crucial point is the hair. Besides the term *ghulam* (pl. *ghilman*), which means literally '(older) boy' but can also be applied to a male slave (of any age) and (euphemistically) to a eunuch, the word which appears most frequently in these contexts is *amrad* ((pl. *murd*), literally, 'beardless'; and Abu Nuwas's society, in which shaving was, if not unknown, certainly not generally practiced, considered the appearance of the beard to be *the* criterion for the transition from the status of non-man to man." Only on one occasion did Abu Nuwas show that he was still attracted to, and tempted to seduce, an adolescent who had already acquired a beard. And he was fully aware that he had played the role of catamite to other men when in his youth, making light of the fact on one reported occasion. In the market place of Baghdad he encountered one Badr al-Juhani al-Barra' in the company of some youths (*ghilman*). Abu Nuwas greeted Badr but was not recognized, at first; the poet enquired about the youths and was told they were Badr's sons, at which Abu Nuwas joked wryly, having divulged his identity, "If I had stayed with you these would now be my children!"

Abu Nuwas's preferred types were adolescent boys employed in the bureaucracy, youths studying religious sciences at the mosque, and Christian and Zoroastrian acolytes. Note must also be made of the *shatir* (pl. *shuttar*), a sort of fashion-conscious dandy of foppish, and occasionally violent, temperament. Being a *shatir* was apparently, Rowson writes,

> ... a "life-style" choice of some rebellious young men (and women), perhaps in that sense to be compared to hippies and punks in modern Western society. There was a distinctive *shatir* "look", as we learn from a description of Abu Nuwas himself, who adopted it (for unexplained reasons) when he traveled to Egypt: "the garb and cut of clothes of the *shuttar*, with his hair in bangs, wide sleeves, and a train to his robes, and covered sandals." ... They are not to be identified with male prostitutes, another group who appear only very occasionally in anecdotes about Abu Nuwas's irregular life.

Abu Nuwas is one of our principal sources on a particular sartorial affectation of early ninth century Baghdad. A number of poems in the erotic section of his *Diwan* devoted to women celebrate the transvestite *ghulamiyyat* — young servant girls and entertainers dressed as young men in svelte and coquettish attire. They wore turbans, close fitting robes and tunics, and sashes; their hair was done up in bangs and side curls, and was cut short at the back to look like boys. The vogue had in fact originated at the caliphal court where it was introduced by al-Amin's mother, Zubayda, in order to distract him from his fascination with the eunuchs of the palace; he was known to have been particularly infatuated with a eunuch called Kawthar. Among the numerous allusions to the *ghulamiyyat* in Abu Nuwas's poetry some are quite witty, for instance the following line which seals a wine poem with the description of a youth: "He is called Ma'n but if you 'turn him round' [or turn it, i.e. the name, around], then it is as if you call his sister, for his name when inverted is Nu'm." This is a clever, and more restrained, variant on the poet's most famous descriptive line about a *ghulamiyya*, to wit, that she has two lovers: a fornicator and a sodomite. The "turning round" or "inverting" of the name is a metaphor for something else, and rather than a brother and sister being involved it is clear we are dealing with a single individual. The cult of the *ghulamiyya* explains the line.

In al-Isfahani's (d. 971) redaction of the *Diwan*, a preamble to the homoerotic poems (*mudhakkarat*) explores a curious prejudice: that homosexuality was imported to Abbasid Iraq from Khurasan, the province which had fomented the Abbasid revolution. Until the end of the Umayyad period, he states, male poets celebrated only female loved ones. "With the oncoming of the Black Banners from the East, they [poets, soldiers, or men in general – it is not clear] began to practice sodomy due to their contact with adolescent boys" (without demur, love and sexual practice are considered to be one and the same). Jahiz, the great polymath of the ninth century, had an explanation for this: the Umayyads took their women with them on campaign, while the Abbasids did not. Homoeroticism, according to this view, is a physical confusion of heterosexual love: "These men, who kept the continuous company of adolescent boys, day and night, would cast their gaze upon a cheek like a woman's cheek, or upon an effeminate leg or buttock; feelings were thus stirred up to such an extent that they might be forced to copulate with a beast or relieve themselves with the palm of the hand. These men returned from their travels with this appetite now instilled in them, exacerbated by the fact that the material costs are negligible and that they could thus avoid the risks of siring children." (D. iv, 141–2) Al-Jahiz ascribed the same practice, and the same underlying causes, to "Masjidites" (men who spent time discussing religion and theology in the mosques) and the men and adolescent boys of the secretariat.

Al-Isfahani peddles these sociological opinions of al-Jahiz (and his own) without any reference to the literary aspect of the poems he is introducing. Rather he tries, unconvincingly, to suggest that Abu Nuwas had been "respectable" and restrained when he wrote under the aegis of Harun al-Rashid but then allowed his sexual profligacy to come to the fore under the license and mutual influence of al-Rashid's licentious son and successor, al-Amin (d. 814). Just as there is a continuous cycle of moods in a single author's poetic biography, where libertine themes arc towards respectability and pious contrition then flounder occasionally in weak moments of recidivist decadence, so al-Isfahani maps out a similar recurring cycle upon history: al-Rashid (upright) ➔ al-Amin (sexually decadent/ homosexual) ➔ al-Ma'mun (upright) ➔ al-Mutawakkil (decadent/homosexual). There is certainly a complexity of moods in Abu Nuwas, but one is hard pushed to establish a chronology for his poetry in accordance with these moods. Al-Isfahani's preamble would seem to be more apologetic than seriously epistolary or discursive.

Character and Temperament

"I sat before a boy who was as lean as a sword
  With the mirage of desire flickering on his cheek,
And I formed a rank in prayer all to myself ...
Now, if I cannot find an excuse for this on Judgment Day,
  I should be in mourning already for wit and charisma." (FP, 174)

Abu Nuwas was outspoken, blunt, and heedless of conse-
quences; thus he was as celebrated by some as he was found irk-
some, and at times dangerous, by others. His frank incitement,
"Give me wine, and tell me: '*This is wine!*' Do not be furtive
while it is possible to be open," provides the measure of his
social and poetic temperament. He was a child both of his time
and his particular upbringing, which straddled the old and the
new, the desert and the metropolis. He could poke fun at himself, scorning his sometimes hapless amorous adventures, but
he saw himself in stature as the successor to the Ancient poets,
and he suffered no illusions about his extraordinary talents: to
his friend 'Amr al-Warraq he boasted sharply and pithily: "I am
unique. Many recite poetry like you."

If this was churlish and mean, he was generous in other
ways and was known to share financial gifts won at court with
other poets who had emerged empty-handed. Ibn al-Mu'tazz,
a formidable judge in literary matters, said of him that "for all
his knowledge and training in the religious sciences he was a
libertine and a profligate; however, he had an immense saving
grace: he was witty and charmed people with his elegance,
grace, amenity, and the diversity of his playful *esprit*. He was the
most generous of men and unstintingly giving." The penury he
frequently experienced as a consequence is shown in some
lighthearted poetic reflections.

Abu Nuwas was also religiously tolerant in a broad sense. He
treated Jews and Christians with much sympathy in his verse, on
rare occasion even affecting to prefer their "authentic" religion.
Yet this posture was tongue-in-cheek since he was no apostate,
and he was at some profound level unshakably a Muslim despite
sundry irreverent remarks and witticisms. His guardian, one
Zakariya' al-Qushari, once remonstrated with him that he could
find no copy of the Qur'an in his house. His answer was: "Light
and darkness are no bedfellows!" Another time in an unsavory
locale, he attended the dusk or *maghrib* prayer, placing himself in
the front row. The prayer-leader began reciting Sura 109 "O ye
unbelievers! – " To which Abu Nuwas responded: "Here I am!

(*labbay-ka*)!" This is provocation, not unbelief; and it is at root no different in motive to his endearing caution about a Persian "heretic" (*zindiq*): "Beware the face of 'Ubbuwayhi! It is the book of heretics! // It contains things – so people say – that entice the heart". All this is *mujun* (the category of dissolute and profane verse or anecdotage that overlaps substantially with bacchic, erotic and satirical materials.)

The complexity of the poet is evinced by the coexistence of poetry in a solemn register, both elegiac and ascetic. It is probably a fallacy to assume, as do some literary histories, that Abu Nuwas composed his ascetic pieces at some point towards the end of his life. Rather, he seems to have composed them throughout his career, stimulated as much by particular events and the varying demands of patronage. Some anecdotes give us insight into this fact, providing evidence of the sort of occasion which may have given rise to melancholic, even God-fearing poetry. One ascetic poem was recited, perhaps even extemporized,[2] at a funeral when an intimate friend was lowered into the grave: "Where are all those who came before us, the strong and influential? ...They have set off on their journey ahead of us and we follow on closely behind ... Death works in an instant, before the blinking of the eye. Tomorrow lying in shabby clothes of dirt and clay, evicted from palace domes and well-built halls, [we] will be unable to come out and play and chatter into the night ..." (*D.* ii, 165)

He was knowledgeable in matters of theology though rarely reverential about them. On the debate between the Jabriyya and the Qadariyya (those who believed in or denied God's determination of events, respectively) he wrote sardonically: "Which of the two is right? – only death and the grave are

---

[2] There is enough cumulative evidence that Abu Nuwas composed his poems on paper, taking care and time in the process. This renders problematic the issue of whether he was able to extemporize as well; a fair number of anecdotes would suggest that he could, but in most cases the poetry that is produced is short or somewhat occasional in nature.

true!"To an approach by the theologian Ibrahim al-Nazzam that he convert to the theological school known as Mu'tazilism, he retorted with a jeer; and he alluded disparagingly to the same man on other occasions, e.g., satirizing his tediously pedantic ponderings on the stillness and motion of objects. Questions of theology and dogma interested Abu Nuwas less than the facetious view that he risked Hellfire – certainly – but might avoid damnation through the all-effacing grace of divine forgiveness. This was an important theme in his wine songs and it was often accompanied by statements of remorse in the recurring aftermath of sin and indulgence. Abu Nuwas was not irreligious in the sense that he belonged to a heretical group. His license with religious pre- and proscription was affected irreverence, as was in essence his reliance on God's clemency as a pliant excuse. It is significant in this respect that the two non-canonical prophetic traditions told on his authority deal with the possibility of entering Paradise as a sinner.

His transgressions were not only those associated with wine-drinking and affection for young men. He could affect to flout the protocols of Ramadan: of all the months, if he could "kill one off", he would dispatch this sacred month of fasting. On another occasion he was more ambiguous (yet still patently mischievous) about "stealing" a breakfast; when Ramadan was about to begin at the end of Sha'ban a friend of his urged that they break their fast early when it started, at which Abu Nuwas rhapsodized: "We will steal a day from our month of fasting; but God does forgive even the thief!" He played with sacred formulae, such as the call to prayer: "Come to prayer!" is rendered, in one profane turn, "Come to sleep-together!" He could put irreverent words in the mouths of others, typically in satire; teasing the Barmecides for their avarice, he had them say: "There is no God but bread!" (parodying the Islamic testimony of God's unity). In an ebullient exchange with the Baghdadi singing-girl 'Inan he wrote: "Gorgeous one! – God has made your face a *qibla* for me, / So allow me to pray toward your face, and lets have a kiss." Here "kiss" (*qubla*) and "the direction of prayer" (*qibla*) are made to rhyme, an almost inevitable rhyming couplet.

There is so much of this kind of pithy anecdotage about Abu Nuwas that it literally fills up two medieval books. Many of the stories will have been falsely ascribed. Furthermore, one must caution: it is too easy to have an exaggerated sense of their intended effect and their actual significance.

Prison

Along with so many figures in the Arabic tradition from pre-Islamic to modern times, Abu Nuwas composed poetry while under lock and key. Much of this contains pleas for release, seeks pardon for moral misdemeanors and warrants new-found contrition. Yet, giving astonishing insight into the poet's nerve and perhaps showing that incarceration was not such a serious matter, nine poems were written in prison celebrating the kind of indulgence he was simultaneously claiming to abandon. The following complaint sets perhaps the smuttiest tone about the poet's detainment: "al-Amin, I languish in the sodomites' prison and fear being buggered. Do you wish them to bugger your very own poet?"

It is certain that Abu Nuwas was imprisoned at least once by Harun al-Rashid and once by al-Amin. Al-Rashid may well have imprisoned him twice, in fact. On the first occasion he was charged with heresy, and on the second with causing offense to the caliph (and much of the political elite) in a famous ode satirizing the Northern Arabs.

The heresy charge is variously related. It is said that he composed an elegy questioning the Hereafter since no one had returned from there to confirm its existence. His friend Yusuf ibn Daya warned him that his many enemies were stalking him for just such an indiscretion in order to precipitate his demise; he begged him to conceal the verses but Abu Nuwas refused to listen. A week later the poet sat in jail.

That al-Amin should have imprisoned the poet is at first sight more puzzling, given that Abu Nuwas is known to have pandered to the debauched interests of the young monarch. Yet historically, and in a more serious political vein, in 810 al-Amin broke with his half brother al-Ma'mun, who governed distant Khurasan and had his eyes on the caliphate. Al-Ma'mun preached against, and probably exaggerated (as historiography has in general), the hedonistic vices of his sibling and from the pulpit in Khurasan the decadent al-Amin was denounced, among other things, for drinking wine with the "dissolute" Abu Nuwas. Al-Fadl ibn al-Rabi' is then said to have advocated his imprisonment. According to other sources al-Ma'mun was himself an admirer of Abu Nuwas.

We must not lose sight of the fact that Abu Nuwas remained a companion of al-Amin. And even though Abu Nuwas's relationship with Harun al-Rashid was conceivably always in the end overshadowed by the threat of punishment, it should be noted that his most famous (and undoubtedly fictional) encounters with this sovereign were essentially frivolous. These are the stories in the *Arabian Nights* which tell how the caliph secretly watched a woman bathing then attempted to render what he had seen into verse. However, stymied and uninspired, he summoned Abu Nuwas to complete his poems. The poet extemporized with sleek, "tender and allusive" eloquence, provoking the reaction from the caliph that his courtier must have been spying on the woman too. Abu Nuwas defended himself by claiming that the caliph's inchoate lines of poetry contained their natural complement.[3] These are the fine ornamental words Abu Nuwas produced about the bathing woman (trans. Eric Ormsby):

> She took off her robes to bathe
> And quick blush reddened her face.

---

[3] In popular stories Abu Nuwas came to be seen as having something of a sixth sense, a quality originally implicit in the Arabic term for poet, *sha'ir*.

Before the breeze she stood, naked,
 Slim-figured, more delicate than air,
and stretched out her hand like water
 To the water that stood in the ewer.
But when she finished and was eager
 To hurry into her garments again,
she saw an onlooker draw stealthily near.
 She let down a darkness over her radiance,
daybreak disappeared under night,
 While water kept on trickling into water ...
Glory be to God who fashioned her
 The loveliest of women on the earth.

Sojourn in Egypt

Abu Nuwas lived in Egypt between the years 805 and, probably, 807, during the tenure of al-Khasib ibn 'Abd al-Hamid as
Harun al-Rashid's fiscal governor. The reasons for his move
there are variously given. He may have been lying low in this
period, having angered al-Rashid with verses lamenting the
fallen Barmecides (he had not been their favorite poet at court,
as we have seen, but the brutal manner of their demise fostered
some verses of genuine compassion). He may also have been
attracted by the prospects of a comfortable income away from
the Abbasid capital. Realistically, he was always bound to return.
 Several anecdotes survive of encounters during his initial
journey to Egypt. In Hims his imminent arrival was conveyed
to the poet al-Batin Sa'id ibn al-Walid. When Abu Nuwas's
arrival was finally announced al-Batin made his way to the tavern and found a man sitting on the steps, decked in a saffron-
dyed sash and holding cake in his hand. "Where are you
staying?" Abu Nuwas was asked; "Is it not obvious?" came the
reply. The Hakamite ended up spending several days in the
company of the local poet and was given an escort for several
miles when he eventually departed. This endearing but otherwise inconsequential story does at least show that Abu Nuwas's

reputation had reached far beyond Baghdad at this stage in his life. The effect of his renown on other poets of Hims was much more intimidating.

In Damascus the people gathered around the poet, requesting him to recite some of his poetry; he recited one *Farisiyya* (poem with Persian vocabulary), but declined to recite any more, declaring bluntly that the people didn't really deserve it! Abu Nuwas did not suffer fools gladly. It is said that when he arrived at al-Khasib's court he dismissed the local court poets claiming that his own eulogies would be "like Moses' staff, crying lies to their deceitful concoctions (*tulaffiqu ma ya'fikun*)". In this caustic put-down Abu Nuwas toys with Qur'anic vocabulary (e.g., an image in Sura 26), and the poem, if not the anecdote, rings true given the way he often spun his poetry from Qur'anic idiom. (The image of the staff is essentially the element around which this story has been woven. This is clear since another story tells of how Abu Nuwas quelled an angry mob in Cairo with four verses warning the people that al-Khasib would consume them just as Moses' snake had consumed the snakes of Pharaoh's sorcerers.)

Death and Afterlife

Four different accounts of Abu Nuwas's death survive: (1) He was poisoned by the Nawbakht family, having been framed with a poem satirizing them. (2) He died in a tavern drinking right up to his death; this is perhaps too easy a reflex and may result from posterity's wishful thinking, enacting the pleas of many of the great wine poets, especially Abu Mihjan al-Thaqafi (d. c. 637), that they should drink until death (and where possible even beyond it). (3) He was beaten by the Nawbakht for the satire falsely attributed to him; wine appears to have had a role in the flailing emotions of his final hours (3 seems to be a combination of accounts 1 and 2). (4) He died in prison, a version which contradicts the many anecdotes stating that in the advent of his death he suffered illness and was visited by friends (though not in prison). He most probably died of ill health, and equally probably in the house of the Nawbakht family, whence the myth that they poisoned him. He was buried at the Shuniziyya cemetery on the Tall Yahud along the banks of the 'Isa canal.

His posthumous status in the literary and popular imagination is unique. The ribald but eloquent and sharply witty figure he cut even during his lifetime survived and was amplified after his death. He thus survives as a character in a number of stories in the *Arabian Nights*, where he is cast as a boon companion of Harun al-Rashid. Many modern Arabs, incidentally, not counting literary specialists or their like, know him, or his 1001 Nights persona, as "Abu Nawas" or even "Abu Nawwas". The anecdotes told about him in popular literature have their seeds in the biographical anecdotes that survive about him, but they exaggerate and distort his traits. He features in Swahili folklore and among the people of Zanzibar he is know variously as Kibunwasi, Bunwasi, Banawasi, or Abunwasi. W.H. Ingrams tells us: "Banawasi has become a proper name meaning 'a man who always has an answer ready, who excels in repartee – a man in fact who laughs best because he always laughs last.'" In the West we have seen what this Abu Nuwas looks like, as he features (though his name is never given) in one of the adapted tales from the *Arabian Nights* in Pier Paolo Pasolini's *Fiore delle mile e una notte*.

Abu Nuwas is all too easily remembered exclusively as a "ritual clown" and for his bacchic and homoerotic poetry, and, at the other extreme, for the more mainstream eulogies and satires. But the creative and mercurial charm of the man seems to lie as much in the cumulative effect of such as the following anecdote: he once traveled with Waliba ibn al-Hubab from Kufa to Hira, on something of a poetic pilgrimage. They trekked there by foot; sinking into the sand with each step and feeling hungry, Abu Nuwas extemporized: "Would there were six loaves of bread between us, and among them a choice goose!" Waliba took the cue and continued the poem: "A Chinese goose, well-grilled and followed with succulent rice!" And so they went on, gastronomy giving way to connoisseurship of wine, their reverie only finally being pricked by arrival at Hira. Abu Nuwas could refashion the world in poetry, and the world he created and inhabited was both real and imaginary. The medieval compilers of his life stories too created a largely imaginary world which we cannot but inhabit a part of it when we reconstruct his life.

2

"LOVE, WINE, SODOMY ...
AND THE LASH"

The Lyric Poetry of Abu Nuwas

"When my eyes roamed his cheeks as if grazing
  In the Gardens of Eternity, he said to me,
'Your gaze is fornicating with me!' I replied:
  'Then my tears will give it the lash above
  and beyond the legal prescription.'" (D. iv, 196)

"I have exhausted the expression of a lover's grievance ...
  I have turned the horizons of speech inside out ..." (D. iv, 144)

EROTIC POETRY

The love poetry (Ar. *ghazal*) of Abu Nuwas ranged in tone from
the sublime to the ridiculous. While he is often remembered
for a bawdy register of poetry that could shatter all literary
strictures of decorum, his chaste love poems at their finest
can be deemed second-to-none in the Arabic tradition. Like
much of his verse in other genres, because he composed so
prodigiously, a lot is cast from a purely conventional mold. Yet
even here a certain poise and mastery is shown, and these
poems should in any case be judged according to a combined
prosodic and linguistic aesthetic that is almost entirely imper-
vious to (anything but the most ingenious) translation. All these
lyric poems – the marvelously original and the quite ordinary

— were in fact also songs, as "lyric" of course connotes, and did not require, in each and every case, distinctive explorations of theme or sentiment. However, across well over 500 poems and fragments of erotic verse, there are indeed numerous images of either extraordinary delicacy or striking, at times seemingly irrepressible invention.

Two Traditions of Love Poetry — A Sketch

By the dawning of Abbasid times in the mid eighth century, Arabic love poetry had developed in two, some argue three, principal ways. Disengaged and separated from a complex, multi-themed and ritualized pre-Islamic ode (*qasida*), it evolved in the seventh century into two "independent" genres: (1) *'udhri*, or chaste and "platonic", and (2) *ibahi*, or sensual and erotic, love poetry. They were both, however, quite dependent on a common stock of descriptive imagery and certain standard motifs (for instance, those of the bestiary of love: the gazelle-like aspects of the paramour).

'Udhri takes its name from the Banu 'Udhra, an Arab tribe from a valley in the northern Hijaz most associated with this kind of expression. *Ibahi* in Arabic simply means "permissive". *'Udhri* poetry proper, which is essentially a phenomenon of the desert, was relatively short-lived — though it had a far-reaching influence through the ages upon Arabic courtly love; the chaste verse of al-'Abbas ibn al-Ahnaf (d. 808), favorite of Harun al-Rashid, assumed the mantle of the *'udhris* in the Abbasid capital, Baghdad. *Ibahi* poetry, associated principally with the Meccan dissolute 'Umar ibn Abi Rabi'a (d. 712), is a poetry of seduction. Though certainly more urbane than *'udhri* verse, it is not yet entirely urban. Some of the more memorable narrative-poems are set in the desert, in a Bedouin context.

There had been some precedents for the intensity of *'udhri* poetry in pre-Islamic Arabia. But it was nevertheless essentially distinctive in several respects. The influence of Islam can be felt in the language and imagery of the new genre (assimilating religious practice into a quasi-spiritual enterprise), and even more significantly in its changed perspectives of time and reality. The *'udhri* poet was an introspective individual; he had a subjective view of the world which he observed through the filter of his love and suffering. The outer world, according to the way he viewed its landscape and fauna, was internalized in psychological harmony with him. The poet devoted himself faithfully and exclusively to one beloved, thus his name is seldom mentioned without evocation of his female counterpart: Jamil-Buthayna, Majnun-Layla, Kuthayyir-'Azza, *et al*.

When love was blighted by time and separation, the pre-Islamic poet had tended to "cut the ropes of affection" (to cut his losses in an heroic posture); the *'udhri* poet, by contrast, projected his love into the future opened up by the new religion: toward death and, of course, far beyond it.

The *ibahi* poet too had precedents for some essential features in both early and late pre-Islamic verse. The philandering 'Umar ibn Abi Rabi'a modeled himself partly on Imru' al-Qays (*fl*. early sixth century). 'Umar's animated poem in which he describes a nocturnal visit to his beloved's tribe (stealing into her tent, spending the night and oversleeping, and having to escape the encampment at dawn draped in a woman's robes, trailing them behind him to erase his tracks), expands upon a short passage in Imru' al-Qays's *Mu'allaqa* ("Suspended Ode"), one of the archetypes of the ancient corpus.

Abu Nuwas was a product (in very schematic terms) of this essential dichotomy of love poetry. Like the verse of the highly influential Bashshar ibn Burd (d. 784) before him, his *ghazal* was an alloy of the various tones and registers in which he was no doubt apprenticed during his literary schooling. Since he is better known for his licentious verse (which in its most depraved mode is scarcely "love" poetry at all), it is worth surveying briefly, as we do in the next section, the possible idealism of his expression. Quite apart from adept allusions to *'udhri* style and technique, pointed references to *'udhri* poets themselves are numerous: we find across poems 'Urwa ibn Hizam, lover of 'Afra', Jamil ibn Ma'mar, lover of Buthayna, and Qays ibn Dharih, lover of Lubna listed almost prosaically. The pre-Islamic proto-'udhri Muraqqish "the Elder", lover of Asma', is mentioned in the same spirit. These references pay lip-service to a certain kind of acute sensibility and create a sense of literary heritage and pedigree.

The range of registers in Abu Nuwas is complemented in an important way by the fact that he composed homoerotic as well as heterosexual poems. In the editorially permissive recension of al-Isfahani there are over 450 homoerotic poems (Ar. *mudhakkarat*), a figure that is something of an exaggeration: al-Suli considers some of them falsely attributed and others to belong in the category of *mu'annathat* (poems written about women). Often they are in fact poems in which the paramour apostrophized or described might be of either gender. This highlights the ambiguity of gender in much classical Arabic love poetry, a feature with its roots in the earliest extant corpus; Abbasid poets could toy deliberately with this elusive facet of gender.

A Digest of Idealized Love

Even in poems where there is an underlying physical sensuality, the description often forms a tissue of sublime imagery. A "gazelle" might thus be

> Created not of clay, like mankind, but rather of musk and other assorted perfumes, brought up in Paradise (Jannat al-Khuld) in the company of black-eyed Houris. (FP, 109)

The beloved is other-worldly and somehow literally angelic, or a statue fashioned to be worshiped in the *mihrab* ("prayer niche").

And when not quite angelic the poet's object of affection may yet be of a preternatural sensibility, physically injured by the merest glance or menacing pointing of a finger

... which almost drew blood from a cheek, exquisitely formed from silver
(D. iv, 381)

The beloved has the powers of Solomon to call upon birds that approach him submissively. Powers of enchantment are conveyed otherwise through a paradox peculiar to music: the singer-lover, imbued with a balanced sense of *dunya* and *din* (the material and spiritual worlds, respectively), has complementary powers both to move and to still: to sway the body of the rapt listener with song and, by the same token, to instill an inner quiet and calm.

Within this realm of the ethereal is the assimilation of language, and even a certain kind of spiritual experience, from religion – a feature of love poetry with roots in the *'udhri* tradition. The darling described in the following poem is barely of this world; he is a gazelle whose

... Eyes deal out among the people their allotted time
... Even [the mystic prophet] Khidr would answer his prayer
And ransom himself for him;
... His place in the next world
Must resemble his place in this;
If we were ever to deny God
We would worship him instead;
It suffices for me that the darkness of night
Envelops both him and me. (D. iv, 150–51)

Assimilated from religious language in a distinct way is any one of numerous adaptations of the Muslim testimony to God's unity – variants of an erotic *tahlil*.[1] The following example (the final tercet of a poem) is burlesque and warps the idealistic tone of the preceding lyricism:

...When he appeared I thought him to be like the crescent moon[2]

---

[1] The *tahlil* is the Arabic credo, "There is no god other than God."
[2] Among the motifs rendered bland with repetition is that of the beloved as the full or crescent moon and the sun. But these belong to a

> And called out, "My Lord (and your Lord), O God!"
> He asked, "Do you then see a crescent moon?" I replied,
>   "If you are not [physically] that, then you are its very sense."
> Beauty had inscribed upon his forehead,
>   "I testify that there is no comely one other than him"
>   (D. iv, 370)

One must read vigilantly to gauge fully the poet's tone. Even from a setting that is awkward for the poet, as on one occasion when accused of seducing his sweetheart's messenger, he manages in fulsome denial to salvage sentiment worthy of true love:

> ... If I flirted with your messenger, the fingers of the Grim
>   Reaper will never clinch my soul!
> Sweet one! Love for you possesses me; I cannot have
>   Two hearts – One preoccupied, the other one blithe. (FP, 33)

Yet one *can* spot a mote in the eye of pure affection. Observe the ending of the next poem (which develops the pre-Islamic motif of the beloved's apparition before the poet in his sleep – the captivating notion of the "*Tayf al-Khayal*"):

> Our two night-spirits meet up when we sleep
>   And union is established as before.
> Sweet balm of my eyes! Why are we wretched
>   While our spirits experience rapture?
> Kind to me in sleep, if you wished
>   You could complete the kindness when awake;
> We are two lovers who enjoy narcotic bliss
>   Yet who are always angry come morning!
> Dreams are deceptive in this way
>   ... But they do sometimes tell the truth. (D. iv, 347)

There is a discreet change in tone, a twist even, in the final hemistich: a possible turn (away from suffering) is implied that

poetic code; Abu Nuwas's originality within this repertoire could be surreal, at once intense and amusing: "My friend, I saw the sun walking about on Friday night // People stirred in wave after wave thinking this marked the Apocalypse; // For the sun to be seen at night! – and they all collapsed to the ground in terror ...."

has both earnest and playful potential. In this respect it is typical of Abu Nuwas; he could derail complacency in ways that were either scandalously graphic or almost, as here, imperceptibly slight.

And the expression of profound feeling, although alluring, can be enigmatic; no more so than when Abu Nuwas steals a look into his sweetheart's face and glimpses his own. Is it the beauty of a burnished complexion that is suggested? Or the threat of violence, a prying glance being caught and returned at the poet's expense? Or, less menacingly, the promise and dawning of reciprocated affection? Our failure to grasp perfectly, despite being captivated by an image, is fitting. In Abu Nuwas's poetry inability to understand is only ever imputed to others. However, this is distinct from lacking powers of description which he contrived intermittently to admit to: "I'll let my imagination describe him since my tongue is flagging." He adds with a frivolous lack of precision, "Only So-And-So and Joe Average (*fulan al-fulani*) could fail to love him." In the most arresting formulation of this kind he wrote: "When it comes to describing him tongues trace their lineage to impotence and failure". Here the inability to delineate is meant to evoke not human failing but a quasi-numinous ineffability: the poet contemplates a sacred darling produced from ethereal light.

Inching Towards Frivolity and Lust

Abu Nuwas once praised the divine hand that fashioned a youth from silver. The hyperbole is at first strained, for the argentine aspect of beauty is not original in this kind of lyric verse. However, what marks the poet's creativity is the way the first line engenders the third (of a three-line fragment): the agent shifts from God as divine silver-smith to the leering poet who is now cast in the role of dyer: for it as if his amorous speech tints with color the cheeks of this youth. In the implied chronology of the fragment (from creation to youthful blush), and within the genre of the poetry, this is an exquisite finishing touch.

There is, of course, frivolity in the intensity of the image. Often the threshold which separates (or merges) the two poetic tempers is reified in a kiss: "I do not wish to take you to bed, or any of that, // All I desire is to speak with you, and to sip and kiss." The most original conceit in this respect is that of a kiss as the outward manifestation of an inner meaning:

> I saw the boy in the darkness and embraced him –
> O would that this kissing could last!
> I kissed him while asleep, if only the true interpretation (ta'wil)
> Of this had emerged when I was awake! ... (D. iv, 240)

The loaded Arabic word ta'wil (used for early scriptural interpretation) renders the consummation of physical desire equivalent, effectively, to the inner meaning of Quranic verses. True love, or sex, becomes apparent with exegesis. Typically, the final line (here the last of only four) sheds most of the affected coyness about what the poet is after: "How lucky the one who can land a kiss upon him; – or garner that which his trousers hold." When refused a kiss by a young man on another occasion, the poet berates him for begrudging him so little yet spraying his honeyed spittle so generously upon the walls (sic); the youth replies that he would grant the poet a kiss if he could be satisfied with just that, but he adds: "We know what you want".

His ghazal could be chaste, decorous, loving, sincere, and intensely emotional (– and mockingly intense: weeping upon the banks of the river Tigris watching a loved one depart by boat he once claims to have raised the water level!). But to be convinced of this solemnity one has to turn a blind eye to the way he could simultaneously undermine this tone. Abu Nuwas often tried to break down the decorum of others in poems braced by chastity but bursting with physical desire. The extreme end of the scale was that of unmitigated obscenity (and profanity). In this respect Abu Nuwas was part of a school of poets with origins in some pre-Islamic verse and elaborated into a veritable sub-genre among poets of Kufa in the mid-ninth century. This is the third genre of love poetry. We already know that Abu Nuwas was apprentice in Kufa to Waliba ibn al-Hubab, one of the arch figures of this group. Risqué elements of poetry are often wrapped within a larger narrative that cushions the shock effect, or even accentuates it as some structural punch-line but shows it in this way at least to be part of a considered craft. Extravagant sexual obscenity for its own sake tends to be a feature of biting satire (where it is indeed common), but there are some examples that are also quite gratuitous in the poetry of *mujun*, for example the occasion, "celebrated" in verse, when the poet met up with four prostitutes who each in turn sung the qualities of her own *pudenda*: "My vagina is like a split pomegranate and smells of ground amber. How lucky the one who gets me when I've shaved!"

His relationship with 'Inan, the renowned "singing-girl" (*qayna*) and one of the women he was infatuated with in Baghdad, was often both acerbic and crude without any hint of complex; he once appealed to her:

Have you yet to find pity for a man yearning,
    Who would be satisfied with just "a small drop" from you?

She replied:

Is it *you* that you mean by this?!
    Be off with you! Go and masturbate!

At which he quipped:

If I do this I fear
    You'll be jealous of my hand! (*FP*, 29)

The Psychology of Master and Servant

> "I fast at your anger and
>   Breakfast at your pleasure" (*D*. iv, 152)

The poet-lover as servant or slave is the predominant image conveying the power relations in this poetry (Abu Nuwas could go as far as saying: "I am to him always like soles are to the shoe!"). Accumulatively this general idea provides the background for, and helps to set up, a game of seduction whereby the tables are sometimes turned. Abu Nuwas's poetry is replete with kaleidoscopic contrasts. It gives a sense of apparently endless variety with limited elements: moods and themes coil around each other in diverse, sometimes antithetical configurations, managed with either abrupt or discreet transitions. Such toying can engender a taut psychological dynamic or cohesion, as illustrated in the relationship between the two halves of a six line poem about attitudes to people and the psychology between two men: (*Note.* The abrupt change of grammatical person, "him" ➔ "you", is known in Arabic as *iltifat* and is a feature of the syntactical independence of the single verse.)

> I wanted to rebuke him for his meanness
>> But then, seeing him and seeing the people [around us],
> I no longer consider it fitting;
>> There is not even a valid point of comparison!
> When I compare you with people
>> I see they are nothing but pigmies and apes.

* * *

> So be proud, my prince, full of arrogance and conceit,
>> Scowl and wear a frown upon your face;
> Pay no attention to people and spare them no thought,
>> Do not even raise your head to them
> And treat me exclusively any way you will;
>> Give me your spurning drink, shun me with every breath!
>> (*D.* iv, 242)

The poet constructs a special place for himself with his darling, importuning him for a monopoly on his scorn. Only in this sardonic way does he feel a cut above the rest while yet a plaything to his princely sweetheart. Acoustically this is a poem that jeers with snarling sibilants at society at large (*al-naSa, Sa'ighan, qiStu miqyaSa, qiStu-ka wa-l-naSa, naSnaSa, wa-Stakbiran, 'abbaSa, al-naSa, raSa, khuSS-ani, bi-ma Shi'tahu wa-Saqqini hajraka anfaSa)*. Such sustained use of onomatopoeia, in which sound and semantics coalesce, is a characteristic effect of the poet.

One of the most original and eccentric of Abu Nuwas's poems elaborates the theme of poet maltreated by his darling in a brutal narrative. It is preserved variously in the chapters of homoerotic and heterosexual *ghazal* by al-Isfahani and al-Suli, respectively; al-Isfahani's hunch has the edge:

> My lover ignored me until, after I had
>   Crossed the flatlands between some mountains
> And had started into an empty desert
>   Wasteland that was bathed in mirages,
> He covered my eyes with a blindfold,
>   Bound my legs with a tethering rope
> And said, "Do not quit this spot –
>   I will protect you against any gossip."
> I replied, "If this happened in my home town,
>   Dwelling of maternal uncles and paternal,
> They would be witnessing my own demise
>   – I had never anticipated such a death!" (D. iv, 299)

This cruel (and erotic?) act of desertion is obscure, though it conveys unmistakably the austerity of an imbalanced relationship between two lovers. It *is* clear that one player, the poet, is prey to the control and domination of the other – the beloved (or "*hibb*" here in Arabic). There are some barely tangible literary resonances that are formalistic and thematic, and also part of the social history of classical Arabic poetry. The desert is bleak and menacing; it is barely described yet the atmosphere of desolation is palpable and betrays a negative investment in this kind of landscape that is something of a piece with Abu Nuwas's often derisory view of Bedouin wastelands. The urban environment is no paradise either, though: here it is the site of lethal gossip – indeed this may be the poem's principal object of attack. However, even this judgment does not inhibit a sense of the narrative intimating at a death-in-love. In this regard it

becomes a somewhat febrile and delirious love poem. It further contains an image perhaps deliberately evocative of a ritual
aspect of pre-Islamic Bedouin burial practice, to wit, the
tethering of a camel to its dead owner's grave. If this effect is
intentional, this is burlesque parody -- and, given the discrep-
ancies in tone between early heroic poetry and this erotic
travesty of it, it emerges as a very wry way of saying how much
poetry has (or should have) developed and moved on since its
pre-Islamic origins. These details are all inconclusive and are, in
one respect, simply intended to retard an anachronistic view
of the scene depicted as an act akin to some modern sexual
practices (though, admittedly, the notion is hard to suppress
altogether: it would be rash to state categorically that Abu
Nuwas is not setting himself up here as some kind of "sex slave"
in a play of "bondage").

In the sphere of emotions which could trap the poet, fear
and submission go hand-in-hand. Fear of the sweetheart's
scorn, certainly; but also real terror, for that is what is evoked
in the cultivated reference of the following line: "He said to me,
his hand in mine after harsh recriminations // 'Do you love
me?' I replied to him, 'Is fear not better than love?'" This
requires a gloss. When the brutal and sanguinary Umayyad governor of Iraq, al-Hajjaj ibn Yusuf (b. 661), asked a man who
had kept his company for a while, "Do you love me?" he replied,
"Is fear not better than me loving you?" As al-Isfahani explains
dryly in his commentary to the *Diwan*, "You obey the one you
fear more than you do the one you love."

Turning the Tables

Young men assembled,
  Sterling coins at the count
    To whom chance time delivered me
"Sunday is close," they said; so I ambled to the promised location
    And was the first to arrive
Dressed like a preacher, in full-covering robes

Kept fast by a plaited cord.
When they had purchased what they wanted,
    Eager to slake their desire,
I approached and offered: "I'll carry this stuff;
    I have the necessary saddle bags:
My ropes are sturdy, and I am brisk and dependable."
"Take it," they said, "You seem to be what you claim
        (*fa-anta anta*),
    And we'll reward you according to your efforts."
So I advanced in their company
    And was told to climb with them [to the spot we were
        making for];
There vessels were unveiled for them (like wives exposed for
        the first time)·
    While a bird warbled in a melancholy strain.
I skipped up to the glasses, and polished them,
    Leaving them like dazzling snow;
My dexterity impressed the beardless young men
    (Though with my skill I intended no good for them);
I served them without respite wine mixed with water
    — It was as warming and bright as kindled fire —
Until I noticed their heads incline,
    Bent and crooked with drunkenness
And their tongues tied and heavy,
    They now either slept or reclined;
I got up trembling to have sex with them
    (All those who creep stealthily tremble [at the thought]!);
Their trouser-bands stymied my pleasure [at first]
    But then, with subtle art, I untied them
To reveal each man's quivering backside
    Oscillating supply like a green bough.
O for this night which I spent enraptured
    In continual enjoyment and excess,
Making from this to that man,
    Screwing whomever I could find in the house
Until the first one awoke and got up
    Feeling bruised at the thighs;
Then I rose with fear to wake up the others,

Saying: "Do you feel the same thing as me?
Is this sweat we've all been stained with?"
    They said: "It looks more like butter."
And when I saw them now alert
    I went off to relieve myself;
And when the *majlis* came to life anew
    I joined them, as the cups passed briskly around,
Draped in the finest colored robes,
    All spanking new;
.I was asked: "Who are you?" And replied: "Your servant;
    From whom you need fear no rude behavior."
Then I sang a love song, captured by the mood:.
    "O would that Salma discharged her vows." (*FP*, 60–62)

The song evoked in the final hemistich is apparently incon-
gruous and hard to gauge in translation, misplaced here beyond
the normal cultural orbit of this kind of archaic and traditional
verse. The point of its inscription is that, despite its brevity, it
strikes a clamorous chord of lamenting and elegiac love poetry. It
represents a genre and tenor of poetry which is anathema to the
one spun out in Abu Nuwas's sexual drama of disguise and recognition. The effect is a bit like inserting a line from Wagnerian
opera into a Vaudevillian song: Abu Nuwas holds horseplay up for
comparison with the earnest, and even tragic, love of archaic
legend (and which, in early Abbasid times, was still the predominant contemporary taste). The extent of the poetic discrepancy,
and the chasm that separates what "the servant" claims about
himself and the abuse he has visited upon his "masters", shines a
glaring light upon the obtuseness of men who have failed to grasp
what has been done to them. It is just one instance of where the
tables of "slave and master" are turned.

The psychology of master and servant is quite different in a
poem we might entitle *The Rescue of Hafs's Pupil*, a narrative that
transforms stock themes and motifs into a unique drama of
cameos. Hafs ran a school for boys in Kufa.

I caught sight of a figure
    Who irradiated disdain.

He was sitting on a prayer rug
　　Surrounded by slaves;
He threw a glance at me,
　　Hunting with his eyes.
That was in Hafs's schoolroom
　　– How lucky is Hafs!
"Take him away", Hafs said,
　　"I find him too silly;
He has not stopped skiving
　　Since he began to study."
Silk robes were stripped from him
　　And a striped garment,
Then they "terrorized" him with molly-coddling
　　Castigation, without even a stick;
Then my sweetheart cried out:
　　"Sir! I'll not do it again!"
I said, "Forgive him, Hafs;
　　He will be good
At reciting poetry, and study,
　　And what-have-you." (D. iv, 194)

Castigation is a double-edged theme and part of the erotic tension of the piece in which, with perfectly pitched under-statement, chastisement-and-leniency or servitude-and-domination, swap roles with each other.

Pandering (to) Satan

"Reveal your feelings to him,
　　Tenderly ...
　　　　Then let Satan break him" (FP, 68)

Abu Nuwas often reworked the kind of contrary sentiments implicit in this callous goading, contradicting himself within the imaginary span of a single day (or night) and cultivating this for literary effect in short dramatic narratives. The role of the Devil (Ar. Iblis) as pimp, expressed tersely above, is treated more expansively in other poems. In the following we find clear reference to the original moment of Iblis's perversion, as treated in the Qur'an — his refusal to prostrate himself before Adam.

> Incensed and enraged,
>> You have watched malevolently upon mankind;
> You waxed proud when prostrating yourself anciently
>> And split from the flower of those who bowed with you
> When you said, "I cannot abide to bow down, Lord,
>> To a type you have created from clay!"
> You were jealous, for you were formed from smokeless fire
>> [And were] master of the created realms;
> So you gave yourself over exclusively to pimping
>> And strive to string fornicators and sodomites along. (*FP*, 55)

Satan Agonistes. Two of the most developed "satanic"[3] poems sustain animated scenes of considerable length. They are highly charged dramatic and antagonistic dialogues pitting dissoluteness against self-denial. One affects pious contrition, the other brandishes religiosity as a threat. But in the end both are of a piece with the poet's own brand of poetic mischief. Al-Suli rejects the authenticity of the first; the authorship of the latter is in even greater doubt. However, they both undoubtedly smack of the poet's genius and are irrevocably part of his tradition: posterity has fairly perceived their creative affinity with "Abu Nuwas" (as a cultural persona).

> When my sweetheart began to spurn me
>> And his letters and news stopped coming,
> I called upon Iblis and said to him
>> Privately, shedding tears by the bucket:
> "Do you not see I am ruined?
>> — How weeping and sleeplessness have emaciated my frame?
> And how my ardor has intensified? Acute worry,

---

[3] These are playful, at worst mischievous poems and are not evil in the way the word "satanic" might suggest. The mystics of Islam often treated the Devil with some sympathy, according to their system of thought — most famously al-Hallaj (d. 922).

Anxiety and passion have almost killed me ...
All for obeisance to you: I have fulfilled your wishes without
    compromise
And scorned those things you despise;
But if you do not now graft love upon
    My darling's heart – as you are so capable –
I will never more recite poetry or hearken to song,
    Nor will inebriation be the sap of my limbs;
Rather, I will recite the Qur'an incessantly,
    Rising early to study it well into the night;
I will account for myself each year [before God], striving
    toward [His Meccan] Sanctuary
And set aside savings of virtuous deeds!"

*   *   *   *   *

Not three hours passed from that time
    Before my darling came to me contritely
Seeking my affection and company
    (So preferable to his previous scorn!)
What happiness after sorrow!
    – At which my heart almost ruptured;
What grace and bounty! – enormous to me
    Though to Satan it was a mere trifle. (*D.* iv, 216–7)

The Faustian theme is inverted: the poet imposes himself
compellingly (and sarcastically) upon the Devil, with no hint of
Mephistophelian mediation. Little real virtue is displayed here,
of course; rather we encounter the momentum so typical of the
poet's lyric narratives: the contrived movement from abstin-
ence, if only as a looming hazard (fancifully and obliquely
contrived), to consummated physical desire. There is tension
followed by a release of that tension in a vigorous ending. This
dynamic frequently has the feel of a stalling, perceptibly drawn
out, from which the poem recovers in an accelerated and
brisk *finale.*

The movement from resistance to surrender, from fettered
desire to gratification, is at first glance utterly absent from the
second of the two poems (see below). In the majority of cases

in his lyric poetry, when Abu Nuwas affected to don a mantle of
piety he was posturing transparently; this poem pretends to be
a rare exception. We gaze upon the poet's sincerity as through
a glass darkly, straining to see what is obscured by the tantaliz-
ing ambiguity of a dream:

> I slept until dawn, and all the while Iblis
>> Antagonized me, tempting me to sin.
> I saw him climb high into the stratosphere,
>> Then fall chased by a star;
> He tried to "listen by stealth" [to the Divine Assembly],
>> But he was soon cast down by a pelting of stones.
> He then said to me as he fell, "Welcome to a man
>> Beguiled by his penitence!
> What do you say to a well-rounded virgin,
>> Adorned with heavy breasts,
> Whose thick, black hair flows sumptuously upon her shoulders,
>> Like a cluster of grapes?"
> No! I answered. "What then of a beardless youth
>> With quivering, full buttocks,
> One like a virgin behind a silk screen,
>> But with a chest unadorned by jewels?"
> No! "Then a boy who sings
>> And plays music delightfully?"
> No! "So you deem yourself resolute
>> In all such things I have spoken of?
> Yet I have not lost hope of your return,
>> Despite yourself, you fool!
> I am not Abu Murra if you do not rescind;
>> You would be naïve to think so. (D. v, 184)

Abu Murra ("The Bitter One") was the byname of Iblis, as in
English one says Old Nick. There are several Qur'anic allusions
in these "satanic verses". Reference to rebellious demons being
chased from the heavens by shooting stars, as described in
Islamic scripture, is easy to detect. But there is also, and more
essentially, allusion to the dialogue between God and Iblis in
Surat al-Hijr (Q. 15: 32–42) in which the fallen angel asks for
respite until Judgment Day to lead man astray: "I shall deck all

fair to them in the earth, and I shall pervert them all together."
Here one such diabolic temptation is enacted, with the lurking
menace of its success in the poem's aftermath (and upon the
poet's awakening).

Fear of Women and Other Anxieties

The figurative imagery of the sea was often employed by Abu
Nuwas to express, and to exaggerate for effect, a fear of feminine sexuality. The sexual anatomy of women posed a physical
threat as menacing as the turbulent deep and his preference for
men was, or came with time to be, articulated as a form of salvation. But his humor may have been decidedly wry, as it was
his own failures, in one or two instances, that seem to have
fomented this kind of misogynist invective.

He once flirted, probably before 803, with a Barmecide ser-
vant-woman from the palace; she was a *ghulamiyya* whom the
poet addressed in verses that were like "knots of magic" (an image
alluding to Sura 113 of the Qur'an). After wine, at the taking of
which the young maiden balked, desire turned sour (in the last
four lines of the poem): "When we got together I found myself in
the middle of a large sea ... I cried out to a young man, 'Save me!'
And he came to my aid, my foot having slipped into deep waters.
... If he had not thrown me a rope, I would have fallen to the bot-
tom of this sea. After this I swore never again in my life to ride the
sea like some marauder; I would travel only upon the backsides
[of men]." A comparable horror influenced the poet's attitude to
those around him: "I will not go into my neighbor's wife, but
rather my neighbor's son." He chastised one lady in particular
with a tirade of bigoted obloquy: "I will have nothing of
menstrual 'flowers' nor sell a gazelle for a hare ... I will not insert
my hand into the cranny for fear of scorpion or snake."

While at times he pretended to psychological revulsion, at
others Abu Nuwas was scarcely more than clowning around; he
may well simply have been laughing at himself all along on
account of heterosexual misadventures. He was at his most

facetiously self-deprecating after suffering from impotence, which may have resulted on one occasion from the horror of a sexual proposition:

> She looked at me from behind her mask,
>> And watched me in an unsavory way;
> I drew off her veil and lo, an old woman
>> Who had dyed her parting black!
> She flirted with me for a long while
>> Addressing me with words of passion;
> She tried to make "Abu Nizar", my member, stand up
>> But this will not happen before the crow turns grey.

* * *

> How can the old woman's desire to be screwed be fulfilled
>> When my penis will not even stand for nubile [maidens]?
> It is now crooked and curled upon its two ends
>> ... Like a handwritten "*dal*" (*FP*, 105)

The image of the crow is one of several common expressions for saying "never" in Arabic. The letter *dal* is the Arabic equivalent of Latin "d" and morphologically it has the shape of a small inverted "c", though slightly more angular. The image the poet is painting here is simply that of something that is not straight or erect: the old woman's brazen flirtation disgusts the poet, so he claims. But the poet may be posturing, hiding (ironically, because he broaches the matter at all) the more uncomfortable fact of his impotence. We can conjecture the latter on the evidence of another, much longer poem. The opening line is off-beat and memorable, borrowing and warping erotic poetry's own special kind of antagonism:

> My penis has started to shun me;
>> The story behind this is that
> I was in a garden of the Caliph's "Palace of Eternity" ...
>> (*FP*, 80–81)

At the very outset an ephemeral wilting member and "eternity" are placed dispassionately side by side – as a kind of ironic signature. The poem proceeds as a long narrative. After sustained description of the floral garden an account is given of a botched seduction. The wine-servant (*saqi*), a customary object of desire, was handsome "in the Barmecide fashion". The effect was radical: "When I saw [this boy]," the Hakamite tells us, "I said to my penis, whose eyes were shedding tears of sadness: 'If you fail me here I will spend a torrid night!'" To pursue his objective the poet employs a common tactic, waiting for his prey "to be assailed by the messenger of sleep": "I waited patiently and when he had reclined on his side I stole up to him like a scorpion scuttling at angles, creeping along my stomach. I then penetrated his trousers (*sirwal*) right up to the flesh. But I was so excited that I misplaced my spear and he felt the jab in his back. He got up, perplexed at my act of cowardice. He was now on top of me and I called out from under him, cursing profanely. My forehead was pouring drops of sweat like dew, and when I managed to escape his clutches, he threw an apple at my face. It hit me right in the tooth. And so it was that I left empty-handed and deprived, and my penis stood laughing, saying (when the fault was all his) 'So it is when one acts according to conjecture!'"

That the poem is bawdy is as clear as its lewd and comic canvass. It is also tinged lightly with religious profanity in the physical and verbal scuffle of the denouement; the apple striking the poet's tooth in the third line from the end evokes the Prophet Muhammad breaking a tooth at the Battle of Uhud. Is this encounter then a burlesque rewriting of Holy War? If the effect is intended, it is done in radical counterpoint since "conjecture" (*zann*) in the Qur'an, and other Islamic literature, is the baleful and dangerous antithesis of *yaqin*, "certain knowledge" of (and blind faith in) religious truth.

Impotence may not actually be physiological here, but there *is* the ridicule of sexual failure. Real impotence appears to be what the poet once wished upon himself in a three line fragment that is as striking as it is baffling (at first):

I am struggling against my eyes,
  My heart and my penis;

Would that for these eyes I had others
   And another heart in place of my own,
And instead of my penis that of an old man
   Who can remember the days of 'Ad. (*FP*, 59)

'Ad were a pre-Islamic Arabian tribe mentioned in the Qur'an as an example of a people destroyed by God for crying lies to their prophet. Theirs is legendary and ancient history. The Methuselean "sheikh" imagined by Abu Nuwas would presumably, given his age, be sexually abstinent. This then is the dignified and physiologically imposed self-control which in a moment of apparent remorse the poet desired for himself; in fleeting regret he would be impotent for dignity.

Seduction and Rape

"Sweet basil is bound to be plucked." (FP, 67)

Abu Nuwas liked to posture as a wolf in sheep's clothing. Once, having donned the attire of a pious man, he announced his abandonment of degenerate behavior and headed for the company of a *faqih* (religious scholar). But it was not any legal opinion that attracted him in the scholar's work, rather the fact that he was a "lord of beardless youths". Fathers entrusted the education of their sons to this respectable tutor in order to evade, as irony would have it, the influence of reprobate men. Abu Nuwas remarked dryly, it was as if they were fleeing from the heat of battle into the very clutches of death: "I was like a spouse to [these boys] when they were learning their lessons!" He asked sardonically in another poem: "When did you ever see a wolf entrusted to tend the sheep?!"

The most extraordinary example of sexual marauding is described in the following narrative:

Among carousers [strewn around by the effects of drink]
   I spotted one awakening;
He stole up to the *saqi* while the household slept

[And] pierced him with something like a viper – silent predator
    of a snake,
  inflicting wounds beyond remedial incantation;
He prized open the boy's ass with the edge of his "sword",
  Then pierced him to the hilt with the head of his "lance".
As he leaned upon his victim, inclined to one side and
    bent over,
  He kept silence while he screwed, eyes cast down –
I said to him: "No holding back, now!
  Show pity and compassion only where fitting!
Squeeze his balls gently. He is quiet because he likes it
  ... And has been longing to be screwed!
If he were not awake his penis wouldn't be standing, and he
    wouldn't
  – while you fucked him – hold his legs together so tight."
    (*FP*, 71)

Nothing crowds the poet's view, least of all his lewd imagination; he plays here the part of a voyeur upon a scene in which
he more normally pretends to an active role. Is this poem an
example of galling and unsightly self-justification, given the
poet's own antics elsewhere, or is this just candor and realism?
Besides the literary point of such variations upon a theme, we
can wonder naïvely here (and indeed in general) why pleasure
and enjoyment – if that is what they are – are couched in such
violent imagery. Is this really simply part of the psychology of
love and sex – of love, that is, when it is unmasked as lust. And
whose enjoyment is it really that is given expression to here?
The poet's prancing imagination in fact seems to taste its own
vicarious pleasure, while offering a prurient thrill to a still
larger audience of decadent reprobates (*mujjan*). The subject of
this poem is not in fact unique; it is the amplification of a rea-
sonably common theme: the lapses of self-possession and hints
of dissolution after a boy's (or a woman's) refusal and restraint,
recorded in poems of callous seduction: "I said: 'Come, let us
blend the good with the unseemly!' He refused, then played for
time ... then let me have the reins."

Writing (and) Letters

> *I wrote to my darling with lacrimose [ink] upon my cheek:*
> *"O the heat of separation!"*
> *He gestured with his fingers, "We understand [the message]*
> *But there is no way for us to meet." ... (D. iv, 265)*

This writing metaphor is of a piece with the closing, and some-what prosaic, apostrophe: "Oh Jeem and 'Ayn before Fa' and Ra' which complete the name" – Ja'far. Broadly, this kind of reference to script and orthography is common in Abbasid poetry. (In pre-Islamic poetry there had been references to epi-graphic marks along desert itineraries and to the mutable traces of campsites likened to effaced writings in the sand – in contrast with their immutable underlying message.)

The poetry of Abu Nuwas suggests that he sent and received numerous letters. Some would seem to have been genuine love letters, taking the form of poems written for the occasion. Others were simply brief messages or missives. They exhibit varied extremes of sentiment. On the one hand, he could write soliciting a letter in unctuous mood, asking Janan to erase each word of her own writing with her saliva so that when he read it and licked it with his tongue he would be receiving a remote and vicarious kiss. On the other hand, he could seduce her messenger.

There are other aspects to "letters" in his verse, which appear largely to have been occasioned by flirting with the young men of the secretariat. A quite common motif in the poetry of *mujun* is the figurative description of penetration. Sex (with a young soldier, in this case) is depicted thus

> The letter "lam" is inscribed in his "meem",
> Healing him from the effects of death (*FP*, 132)

"*Lam*" is the Arabic letter "l" and has a similar form to the Latin "l", with a cursive lower stroke that arcs downwards and to the left; it is the most erect of the Arabic letters and the connota-tions are obvious. "Meem" is the letter "m" and takes the form of a circle (in certain hands this tends to be small enough to merge as a black dot); the letter has a dipping tail only when it stands alone or at the end of a word. In this line, and others like it, it is clearly the form of a medial "meem" that is intended. The idea of a "lam" inserted within a "meem" is scarcely impenetrable when we consider two men – or a man and a woman – having sex, and needs no gloss. In other poems the letter *ha*' ("h") may be a variant for *meem*. And in one particularly prurient poem the *meem* of a young secretary "throttles the *lam* which it encompasses"; Abu Nuwas may often have been gratuitously anatomical but there is also much realism in his descriptions and so, with the scant evidence he offers, one cannot help but suspect that the boy in question was younger than he should have been. The value judgment, partially anachronistic, is implicit in the physicality of the image. It may appear gallingly cynical that the poet should portray *himself* as the victim of an act of violence, but he would have been the first to be conscious of the cynicism. This is humor laced with dark poetic mischief, and there are some inevitable table-turns of roles: further along in the poem Abu Nuwas has a *membrum* that could "hamstring a she-camel". This is to say, he was hardly ever convincing as the victim of sexual violence.

Variant reference to letters lies in the following, the rude climax of a poem. The scene evoked, half veiled in metaphor, still leaves little to the imagination:

> ... When the tawny wine had taken hold of his mind
>   On this dark and tenebrous night
> He bowed his head ...
>   And I spent the night wakeful;
> If you saw this, my friend – a meal
>   To top all others –
> And how my "pen" was cleaving a "kaf"
>   Into his pale "parchment",
> You would be watching a man
>   Gobbling meat hunted within sacred precincts.
> When the boy awoke and saw what looked like
>   Marrow on the tips of the fingers
> He said: "You did it! ..." (*FP*, 80)

Since hunted within a "*haram*", this "meat" is illicit. The letter *kaf* is tall, sloping and sharply angled in two principal strokes (when medial); it is one of the more visually prominent and majestic in the Arabic alphabet. The word *akkal*, translated here as "gobbling", lays acoustic stress on this letter which is doubled here. The ironic effect of the word thus lying adjacent to the metaphor of the previous line would not have been lost on the poet (even if, conceivably, it were not originally calculated).

In the following two lines about a boy from the secretariat there are *other* connotations in mention of *other* letters. Their significance is less obvious: "He spread the parchment upon his lap, beginning with *ya'* and *sin* ("y" and "s"); // at [the sight of his] handwriting one's breath felt as if constricted between a *waw* and *nun* ("w" and "n")." This requires some exegesis. *Ya* and *sin* are the eponymous Qur'anic "mystical" letters of "Surat Ya Sin" (Sura 36). They are the opening letters of this chapter of the Qur'an; the boy is thus clearly practicing Qur'anic calligraphy and causing those who look upon him in thrall to be short of breath, as if confined in the narrow space between the unjoined letters *waw* and *nun*. These letters occur both in verse 6, *ghafilun*,[4] and the final verse, 83, of this sura: ... *wa-ilayhi turja'un*. The latter phrase refers to death and God, "to Whom you return" (*FP*, 119); the allusion may thus serve to evoke the poet giving up the ghost as a result of gazing upon the skill of this boy – skill inscribed as a metaphor for his physical splendor.

Christian Boys

> "*Is it not considered grave among all who pronounce God's unity*
>   *That a Christian faun should torture a Muslim?*
> *If it were not for the threat of Hellfire*
>   *I would worship 'Isa ibn Maryam instead of God.*"
>   (*D*. iv, 320–21)

---

[4] The *waw* in Arabic is also long "u", depending on surrounding vocalic morphology.

In Arabic the words for "cross" and "dear" or "beloved" are morphologically identical and share a rhyming consonant: *salib* and
habib – a neat mnemonic aid to one of the most salient aspects
of Abu Nuwas's erotic poems: the desire he celebrated for
young Christian acolytes who served in the monastic wine
taverns of Iraq. Inevitably, he made use of this rhyming couplet
on one occasion in lines of playful doggerel:

> By Jesus, the Holy Ghost,
>   And by your veneration of the Cross (*salibi*)
> Halt when you come near us
>   And say Hello, my dear! (*habibi*) (*FP*, 129)

There is much more than this in the *Diwan*. Across numerous
lyric poems, which in most cases blend the bacchic and erotic
registers together seamlessly, Abu Nuwas demonstrates quite
detailed knowledge of Christian scripture, practice and belief,
as well as some aspects of its pastoral hierarchy. Subjects range
from reference to the two Evangelists, John and Luke; the
Psalms and Palm Sunday; the Nativity; and the icons and
iconography of Mary and the Resurrection. He even expressed
admiration for Christian architecture – the marble blocks and
pillars of a Christian monastery or church. A trip to
Masarjasaya, a monastery outside Baghdad, was once dearer to
him than pilgrimage to Mecca.

Inevitably the imagery can be at variance. Sometimes the
object of his fascination "babbles in a foreign tongue". Yet other
times he is supremely eloquent; in a poem whose cohesive
structural syntax is that of comparison ("The kiss of the wine
when the jars prostrate themselves around it in prayer, in a
house of pleasure ... [lines 1–2 ➜ line 11] is more lovely to me
than spring encampments and barren wastes"), a "gazelle
among the Christians ... spills words when he speaks that are
like pearls breaking from their string".

His most famous Christian poem is set in the close vicinity of
a monastery where he observed worshipers on their way to
Mass. It is short (7 or 8 lines in different recensions) yet one of

the gems of the *Diwan*: a vivid tableau that finds its focus in an image of the Eucharist, simultaneously representing both the sublimation *and* disclosure of true desire. Though the context is Christian, it is cross-laced with discreet Qur'anic references. The underlying agenda is profane – superficially it depicts nothing less than a Muslim's apostasy – yet it is far from obscene:

> My body is racked with sickness, worn out by exhaustion:
>> My heart smarts with pain searing like a blazing fire!
> For I have fallen in love with a darling whom I cannot mention without
>> The waters of my eyes bursting forth in streams.
> The full moon is his face and the sun his brow. To the gazelle
>> Belong his eyes and his breast.
> Wearing the belt of the non-Muslim (*zunnar*), he walks to his church;
>> His god is the Son, so he said, and the Cross.
> O I wish I were the priest or the metropolitan of his Church! No, I wish
>> That I were the Gospel and the Scriptures for him!
> No, I wish that I were the Eucharist which he is given or the chalice from
>> Which he drinks the wine!, No, I wish I were the very bubbles of wine!
> So that I might obtain the benefit of being close to him and my sickness,
>> Grief and cares be dispelled!
>>>> (*FP*, 130–31; trans. Montgomery, 1996)

The poet would fall in with the religion of the boy and become its dearest symbols. Yet this is devotional idealism only thinly camouflaging consuming physical desire; for all that the imagery is compellingly sacred it expresses no more, in the end, than delirious hope for an intoxicating kiss. It is, as Montgomery (1996) has written in his fine commentary on this poem, "an allusion to one of the highpoints of the Arab erotic experience, the imbibing of the beloved's saliva which is as potent and sweet as wine."

* * * * *

WINE POETRY

It is a noticeable paradox of literary history that a rich and abundant corpus of poetry celebrating wine developed in early Islamic society despite the Qur'an's ban of its consumption. In later periods, by the eleventh century, it became possible to excuse wine in verse as a purely symbolic figure of mystical expression; and there has been a tendency in modern times to project this kind of symbolism back onto the earliest canon of Bacchic poetry. But this is – on the whole – an anachronism. If Abu Nuwas was a mystic he kept the matter remarkably well hidden from his contemporaries and immediate entourage.

Wine in classical Arabic poetry was a legacy of the pre-Islamic canon. The poets of the *Jahiliyya* ("The Age of Ignorance") celebrated wine as a minor theme in their complex, multi-part odes (*qasidas*). Wine was a theme subordinated to a number of poetic registers, but principally: self-vaunting poetry (Ar. *fakhr*) and erotic poetry (Ar. *nasib* and *ghazal*). It was also in reality a rare commodity. Though there was some local Arabian production of wine in the Hijaz, notably at al-Ta'if, it was on the whole imported from Syria and Mesopotamia, and was therefore considered luxurious. There are scenes described of poets making for a wine merchant's ramshackle stall and spending irresponsibly both their earned and inherited wealth. This was an act both of heroic recklessness, analogous with physical audacity on the battlefield; and it was a gesture of consummate generosity at one's own expense. The early poets also compared, in detailed pictorial vignettes, the saliva of their loved ones to wine and honey (which were often in practice mixed together). These vignettes could be longer than the erotic passages in which they were set, displacing the image of the beloved. Wine in this sense could console frustrated love. But it tended to be as true of wine as it is of love that its enjoyment in pre-Islamic poetry was set in the poet's past as a nostalgic memory.

In the Islamic period wine survived as a theme within the compound ode (*qasida*). However, it also, from the very beginning of the seventh century, became disengaged from other themes and developed into a separate genre – the genre which Abu Nuwas perfected, imparting to the wine song (*khamriyya*) a broad repertory and a literary quality and sophistication on a par with any of the other genres. Disengaging the theme of wine from the *qasida* was in some sense liberating. It gave wine the room to expand its own repertory of descriptive and narrative themes. But it also removed some of the formality imposed by the more formal compound genre (which came to be associated with the protocol-conscious panegyric – see Chapter 3). Wine became a medium of liberated expression, giving voice to verses of religious profanity, hedonism and licentiousness. These became especially apparent in the early eighth century (e.g., among the so-called dissolutes, or *mujjan*, of Kufa) but there are some notable earlier examples. Abu Mihjan al-Thaqafi (d. *c.* 637) was the first poet to challenge Islam in a rakehell posture (of which he later repented, also in verse).

Of course, wine also survived as a theme because it was consumed. It was tolerated by the ruling elite largely for the elite in restricted *milieux* where it neither challenged nor imperiled the religious and political order. The profane poetry of the sort we have read above, and will read below, may have stretched this tolerance to the limit; but that this tolerance never snapped irreparably in early Islamic society suggests the poetry was then less accessible to the public at large than it is in most regions today. Wine was associated in its production and sale with Christian monks, Jewish merchants and Zoroastrians. The wine poetry of the Abbasid period is a corpus full of both fantasy and realism; the latter gives us much valuable information on the viticulture of the day: the locales of production and consumption; the appliances used for drinking; the types of wine (principally from date or grape juice); the habits of drinking (e.g., wine was nearly always mixed with water and often drunk in the early morning); the variety of people involved, i.e., clients, merchants, servants and entertainers. These have all been discussed in detail in Jameleddine Bencheikh's *Poésies*

Bachiques d'Abu Nuwas: Thèmes et Personnages. Some literary aspects of these poems will be concentrated on below. Any reader of the wine songs of Abu Nuwas should have a sense of their mock-heroism; their sometimes rash antinomianism; and the way they assimilate the language of religious experience in a game of parody blended in with some genuine anxiety. The selections and commentary below are influenced by these three aspects (discussed in a famous study by Andras Hamori) and the related facets of his wine poems outlined in Chapter 1: (i) the varied coupling of erotic and Bacchic themes; (ii) two complementary views of time; (iii) the rhetoric of antagonism and contention; and (iv) the ambiguity of apology, contrition and repentance.

Beloved Wine

In a famous line of poetry from the early Umayyad period Humayd ibn Thawr asked (referring to the spectral owl-like bird that was believed to appear on the grave, especially of those murdered and unavenged):

Will the ghostly screech of Umm Awfa call to me
  Once I am but bones and a tomb?

Similarly, in imagining of a time after death, the more cheery 'Umar ibn Abi Rabi'a wrote:

I wish that I, when my death draws nigh,
  Might smell what lies between your eyes and mouth,
That the water with which I am purified
  Might be compounded of your marrow and your blood
And that Sulayma might lie beside me in death,
  Whether in verdant heaven or in hell

Abu Mihjan al-Thaqafi wrote a line of equivalent sentiment, not about his sweetheart but about wine:

If I should die, bury me by a vine
  Whose roots after death may slake my bones' thirst

It is evident from these examples that wine and love were susceptible of similar treatment, influenced by developments in society made possible by Islam: a vivid sense of life after death. The feckless Umayyad poet-cum-caliph Walid ibn Yazid (d. 744), whose moral delinquency is said to have hastened the collapse of his dynasty in the mid-eighth century, shows another facet of erotic bacchism; in a famous fragment he reworked the Qur'anic image of poets drifting deliriously (scilicet, from passion) in "every Wadi" (Q. 26: 226):

How I wish today that
  My share of life's provisions
Was a wine on which to squander
  My earnings and inheritance;
That, infatuated with it, my heart might drift
  In every dry river valley.

These lines are mock-Qur'anic but also mock 'udhri. Taking into account all the above excerpts we see that both licentious love and its chaste counterpart came to be felt in the eroticism of wine poetry. The following lines by Abu al-Hindi, an early contemporary of Abu Nuwas, are modeled on the amorous exploits of Imru' al-Qays; we are at first taken in by the metaphor of embrace until it transpires that the poet has been fantasizing about sipping wine:

I remember smelling a diffusion of musk from a cheek
  Whose fragrance wafted towards us;
So I made my way to see her, when her relatives were asleep
  In the early morning and the curtains had not yet been
      thrown aside to
  Reveal her ...
I kissed her on the bed; she had the fragrance
  Of a perfumist's stone-pounder.
A man who drinks her gives his money away generously
  When the Saqi passes her round in the middle of
      the night ...

Below Abu Nuwas apes the excessive devotion of the *'udhris* without even a hint that this is parody, unless parody lies in the very excess:

> Do not reproach me over wine, my friend,
>> Do not scorn me with a frown for drinking;
> Merciful God has decreed a love for her of me
>> And of those with whom I pass the time;
> My heart has fallen for her, and this passion has made me
>> think little
> Of spending upon her all the valuables I own;
> I have become insane for [this] delicate virgin
>> Who is excessively violent in the glass and headstrong.
> You would consider her cup in the mixing to be decked out
>> In the headdress of a bride;
> She rends the veil of one's heart, provoking
>> Innermost secrets to be divulged. (*D.* iii, 188–9)

Failed Cross-Wooing and an Orgy

The affective intensity of the last piece is rare. The great majority of Abu Nuwas's wine poems are driven by a quest for pleasure, the sense of which could be accentuated by playing his hedonist's compulsion against the melancholy of ancient poetry. The erotic prelude of the pre-Islamic (and later Islamic) *qasida* was mournful and nostalgic (see Chapter 3). Abu Nuwas may well have liked the original poetry but he is famous for mocking the inane aping of its desert imagery and, in his lyric verse, for writings that diverged, often provocatively, from its sorrowful tone.

Below is a poem which is in fact fonder of the ancient poem it alludes to than it is derisive, for its author was one of the two or three most significant forefathers of the wine song as an independent genre:

> Quick to your morning drink and delight yourself, my man!
>> Defy those who boorishly fault your love.

Throw off all shame and amuse [those] that are sad;
  Follow them around wherever they go.
May the light-hearted libertine experience joy
  And an easy life and obtain the good things!
May it rain upon a gathering of youths with whom I carouse,
  Among whom there is no idiocy!
This one is for that one just as this one and this other are for that:
  A gathering all in order, its rope of union utterly intact.
How noble they are, and how noble a singer is Nuʿm,
  For Nuʿm's singing is proverbial,
A slender girl who sings to us accompanied by a moving lute:
  "Say farewell to Hurayra for the riders are about to depart!"
        (*D.* iii, 256)

It is typical of Abu Nuwas to create a narrative cameo of the drinking scene in which a songstress is depicted reciting a poem to music; many *khamriyyat* end this way, quoting a recognizable line of lyric poetry from the pre-Islamic, Umayyad or even Abbasid canon. Here he quotes the first hemistich of Qays ibn Maymun "al-Aʿshaʾs" "Suspended Ode" (*Muʿallaqa*). Al-Aʿsha (a sobriquet meaning the Night-blind) was a late pre-Islamic wandering poet famous for his long and sophisticated panegyrics. It is said that he almost converted to Islam in 629 but fell just short of the act, dissuaded at the last minute upon finding out, already on route to visit Muhammad, about the Islamic proscription of wine. He died soon after the aborted trip, a fact regretted in medieval commentaries, galled at the fact that salvation had slipped through his fingers.

Let us now first of all show the "intertextual" connection between the poems of al-Aʿsha and Abu Nuwas clearly and schematically, before commenting on related themes. Al-Aʿshaʾs *Muʿallaqa* begins:

Hemistich 1: *Say farewell to Hurayra for the riders are about to depart;*
Hemistich 2: *But can you suffer to say farewell, my man?*

Abu Nuwas's poem begins and ends:

Hemistich 1: *Quick to your morning drink and delight yourself, my man!*
Final hemistich: "*Say farewell to Hurayra for the riders are about to depart*"

The first line of the older poem provides the beginning and end of the later one. But is this nothing other than a well crafted tribute to an admired literary predecessor? There is something more to the relationship between the two poems represented physically, as it were, in the inversion between the two elements they share: al-A'sha's

hemistich "a" ➔ hemistich "b"

gives Abu Nuwas's

(evocation of) hemistich "b" ➔ final hemistich "a"

The inversion is a deliberate symptom of the contrastive thematic relationship between the two poems; that is, the energy and exuberance of Abu Nuwas's poem may form a deliberate counterpoint to the solemnity which infiltrates the revelry of al-A'sha's long *nasib*. Al-A'sha restrains his exuberance and that of his companions – an irresponsible quest for pleasure – in order to augur for rain:

> Can you see the cloud which I have been watching?
>   The lightning is like firebrands around its edges ...
> Pleasure did not distract me from it as I watched it,
>   Nor the delights of the cup or other heavy matters.
> I said to my drinking companions at Durna after they had
>   become drunk,
>   "Augur for rain!" Yet how can a drunkard do so?!

Abu Nuwas understood these lines, but his cameo narrative has not yet reached that point in time when responsibility will make a man sober; his central line is thus:

> May it rain upon a gathering of youths with whom I carouse! ...

There is not yet a hint of temperance here; indeed, the sentiment precedes the most succinctly decadent (if not entirely graphic) image in the poem:

> This one is for that one just as this one and this other are for that:
> A gathering all in order, its rope of union utterly intact.

With the vague demonstratives "this" and "that" Abu Nuwas is not so much being mealy-mouthed as acknowledging the inspiration of his tutor, Waliba ibn Hubab of Kufa, who had written in a cheerful poem "This one kisses this other one, and this one here kisses that other!"; it is something of a motif in Arabic literature, as indeed – in world literature – is its very contrary; to wit, the poignantly humorous scene of frustrated "cross-wooing" depicted by al-A'sha in his melancholy *nasib*:

> I was infatuated with her, and she with another man;
> That man with another woman – not her!
> A young girl was in love with him but he had no desire of her,
> While she had a cousin who was dying for love of her, in a
> wretched state;
> Another young girl fell in love with me, but she did not suit me.
> Thus did love come together, all of it insane!

Ben Jonson, for one, transposed this elegantly in *Every Man Out of His Humour*: "... the argument of his comedy might have been of some other nature, as of a duke to be in love with a countess, and that countess to be in love with the duke's son, and the son to love the lady's waiting maid; some such cross-wooing, better than to be thus near and familiarly allied to the times."

Two Views of Time

The religious penitent, characterized standardly as a scrimping miser because of his abstemiousness, feels death to be near and the Hour of Judgment looming after it. His piety is a fear based on an eschatological – Islamic – view of time. The hedonist questions time borrowing the imagery of the ancient poets who felt its passing represented in the abandoned traces of former camping grounds. Often, the Bedouin poet would ask the effaced marks of an encampment where its inhabitants or his loved one have gone (*Ubi sunt ...?*). No answer ever comes from mute rocks, which is as good as an answer for Abu Nuwas: it is useless to question time – far more useful to drink in spite of it. These comments explain the next poem and, to some extent, the one after.

> Stop at the abode of the departed,
> > And cry if you are melancholy;
> Ask the abode,
> > "When did your residents leave?"
> We have asked
> > But it refuses to reply.
> – O Daughter of the Sheikh, give us drink this morning!
> > Why do you linger so?
> A lissome sap runs through you,
> > Now make wine flow through us.
> We only ever drink,
> > Be certain of this,
> That which is anathema
> > To the draught of the pious.
> Turn the wine away from a miser
> > Who has found religion in frugality;
> Time begins to drag on for him
> > So he fears the Hour approaching. (*D.* iii, 316–17)

"Whose Are The Remnants ...?"

In the next poem two kinds of desolation are seemingly incongruously juxtaposed: the painful remembrance of love in a desert wasteland and the forswearing of wine. It is the quality of the poetry throughout (the deft handling of ancient motifs, in part one, and the exquisite description of wine, in part two) that persuades a man forsworn from drinking to abandon his resolve. In this sense the poem is rhetorical.

Whose are the remnants at this place where the riders alight,
    Buried away, traces effaced, all but enduring hearthstones
    Of dark and somber hue?
It is as if melancholy doves have gathered at this dwelling,
    Strangers of an evening, without a nest to go to;
– The abode of a woman [I once knew] whose saliva
    Was sweet and whose touch was soft.
Yet she was unjust! Emaciation is visible on my face
    While [in my mind] her face is preserved from decay.

* * *

Through many [such] a desert in which the wind,
    Blowing through the contours of the land,
Produces a variety of obscure and clear language,
I have urged my pedigree mount on
    Until her eyes were sunken and her belly emaciated.

* * * * *

And I said to one who has forsworn wine, "Have a morning cup;
    One should not make religious oaths [to abstain] from such
        things!"
A fresh wine unvisited by the death-dealing Fates,
    For she has passed years in her jar, and years upon that;
The heirloom and legacy to a people from a people destroyed,
    Inherited by children from those who had been children
        before them;
Those who have survived obtained a final spark of life from it.
    A wine both frisky and quiet [when mixed with water],
As if lines of Himyarite or Persian appear on its surface,
    Which, with time, become almost intelligible,
Amid freshly picked narcissi which
    To our eyes are themselves eyes, though they differ in their
        shape:
    Yellow in place of black, with white lids.

* * *

When [the man forsworn] heard my description
    He gave up his [abstemious] stance, calling me back;

At which I said, "Here's a friend who was stubborn at first
  But then gave in!"
For he believed my opinion about wine, may God condone his
  Whenever he opines well. Opinions are indeed various!
    (D. iii, 305–8)

There is one noticeable connection in the imagery across the
two distinct parts of the poem: the wind in the desert produces
a sound like an unintelligible language while the bubbles on the
surface of the wine seem, with time, almost as decipherable as
writing. Wine is more meaningful. (The description of such
bubbles gave rise to pictures of astonishing inventiveness, none
more so than when the poet imagines he sees an ancient griffon
pulling on its reins. In reality the bubbles may suggest
something far more prosaic: that the wine had not properly
fermented.)

Trumping the Theologian

We discern the same function of rhetorical description in Abu
Nuwas's most famous (and often bowdlerized) *khamriyya*
where the sublime picture of a luminous wine undercuts a
philosopher's condemnation of its consumption.

Do not scold me for it tempts me all the more,
  Cure me rather with the cause of my ill –
A pale [wine] whose house is not visited by sorrows
  Which imparts joy even to the rock that touches it;
Received from the palm of one with a cunt,
    Dressed as one with a penis,
  Whose lovers are two: fornicator and sodomite.
She brought the wine jug on a dark night
  While her face emitted a bright light,
Casting pure wine from the lip of the jug –
  A sedative for the eye to behold;
More gentle than water, which ill suits her delicate [essence] –
  Water is too coarse to blend with her;
But if you were to mix light into [the wine],

It would blend well and generate a multitude of lights;
She was passed around among men by whom Fate was humbled,
　　Men afflicted by Time only as they pleased.
For her do I cry, not the spot at which
　　Asma' and Hind once alighted;
No tent is set up for Durra,
　　No camels or sheep are to roam around her!

* * *

Tell him who would claim philosophy as part of his knowledge:
　　"You have learned some things, but much more escapes you;
Do not deprive [me] of God's forgiveness, if you yourself
　　Would abstain from sin;
　　To deprive me of this would be a blasphemy." (*D.* iii, 2–7)

Asma' and Hind are proverbial names of loved ones in the antique *nasib*; Durra, by contrast, was the servant-girl of Abu Nuwas. Wine is a sensuously feminine entity ("whose house is not visited by sorrow", unlike the proverbial Asma' or Hind), and "she" is described in such a way as to blend in with the cross-dressed *ghulamiyya*: light irradiates blindingly from both.

The poem is famous in medieval texts for the first line and the last two which are directed against the Mu'tazilite theologian Ibrahim al-Nazzam. Among the tenets of Mu'tazilism is that there can be no divine forgiveness for grave sins (*Kaba'ir*), only for relative misdemeanors (*Sagha'ir*).

The luminosity of wine occupies less space but is more significant in the following ...

Dialogue with a Jewish Taverner

Remember true friends whose mounts I led
　　To a taverner's house, arriving at midday;
His "zunnar" girdle told us he was not a Muslim,
　　So we thought well of him though he thought ill of us;
We asked, "Are you of the religion of Christ, the son of Mary?"
　　At which he turned away from us and uttered some foul
　　　　words;

[No he was] a Jew who appears to love you
  Yet secretly harbors betrayal;
We asked, "What is your name?" He replied, "Samuel;
  However, I am known by the "Kunya" Abu ʻAmr ("Father
    of ʻAmr")
  Though I have no son of that name!
An Arab "Kunya" has done me no honor,
  Nor filled me with pride, or given me high rank,
But the name is light and has few letters,
  And is not burdensome like others."
So we said to him, admiring the grace of his speech:
  "You speak eloquently, so do as well with the wine that you
    serve us!"
He turned away, as if to shun us,
  Now looking at our legs now at our faces,
And said, "By God! Had you alighted upon someone other
    than me,
  We would have rebuked you; I will excuse you [now] and be
  Generous!"
Then he brought out an oily, golden wine
  To which we could not help but prostrate ourselves;
We had set out [on our foray] with the intention of spending
    three days,
  But we had such a good time that we stayed a whole month!
A band of good-for-nothings, the likes of which you will never
  see,
  Though I was one of them, neither innocent nor empty of
  blame;
When the time for prayer drew near, you would see them
  Ask for more wine so that it might pass them over in a
    drunken state! (*D.* iii, 130–32)

The *zunnar* was a girdle or sash worn by Christians and Jews
to distinguish them from Muslims according to a dress code
established in the seventh century in the so-called "Pact of
ʻUmar". The *kunya* is the Arabic "cognomen": that is, a construct
name beginning with "Abu" and followed by a forename: thus
Abu ʻAli, Abu Ahmad, etc. It means "father of ..." and is either

adopted by a man after the birth of a first son (the feminine equivalent is Umm 'Ali, Umm Ahmad, etc.), or used as a *nom de guerre*, or a nickname, as in the case of Abu Nuwas, usually high-lighting a person's characteristic feature, physical or abstract. Strictly, *dhimmis* (non-Muslims) were not allowed to adopt Arab Kunyas in the ninth century. Here the situation is peculiar and not entirely clear: the Jewish taverner appears to have had the name Abu 'Amr foisted upon him, perhaps by his easy-going Arab clientele (no doubt insouciant of name restrictions when indulging in forbidden wine). He is in any case ambivalent about the Kunya: for it has done him no real honor, nor changed his situation much, but at least it is not cumbersome. He is proud, no doubt, and the clients admire the way he expresses himself. What we can say for sure is that the discussion of "Abu 'Amr" is an intertextual flourish of the kind Abu Nuwas relished: it alludes fondly to a line from the *'udhri* poet Majnun Layla: (trans. Rina Drory) "My heart refuses to love anybody but an 'Amiriyya (a woman of the 'Amiri tribe); her nickname is [Umm] 'Amr, though she has [no son by the name of] 'Amr". This is the only intimation of an erotic register in the poem.

Vivid and animated dialogue takes the place of elaborate description in this wine song; the result is a narrative cameo of great realism, producing a subtle portraiture of human senti-ments: at first some resentment and then admiration and mutual respect. Here the absent Christians come off as heretics, but the Jewish vintner, at first tarred by a bigoted slur, wins over his Arab visitors with his crustiness and silver tongue (– and then the quality of his wine).

There is one striking descriptive element of the wine that is highly significant, chiming in with both the "antinomian turn" of this poem and its "assimilation of religious language and experience" (the worshiping of wine and flouting of prayer). The epithet "oily" to describe wine is unusual; it might seem clumsy and infelicitous as an epithet for choice wine were it not for the fact that it must surely allude to the Qur'anic "light verse": (Q. 24: 35)

God is the light of the heavens and the earth. His light is like a niche in
which there is a lamp; the lamp in a glass, and the glass like a brilliant
star, lit from a blessed tree, an olive-tree neither from the East nor from
theWest, whose oil almost glows, even though no fire has touched it. Light
upon light. God guides to His light those whom he wishes ...

Lexically, the phrase "*an oily, golden wine to which we could not
help but prostrate ourselves*" contains a direct albeit cursory allusion to the Qur'anic verse, which was such a favorite of the
mystics of Islam (a whole commentary is devoted to the
verse by the great Sunni and mystical theologian al-Ghazali
[d. 1111]).

Numinous Wine

There is a gnostic feel to any such image, a feature that can be
felt more palpably in the entirety of the following poem. It contains the most numinous and idealized description of wine in
the *Diwan*. This makes it extraordinary that Abu Nuwas is said
to have composed it in Egypt while in a sordid state: he collapsed in a drunken stupor, urinated upon himself, and would
have lost the precious poem to oblivion had it not been written
out for him on the walls by the son of his host:

O my brother of the clan of Hakam,
   You slept last night while I lay sleepless,
So pass me the virginal [wine] which has cloaked itself
   In the head scarf of grey locks while still in the womb;
Youth answered to her call
   After she had passed quite beyond old age,
For she is a wine [preserved] for the day when she is pierced,
   Though an edge ahead of Time in years;
She is so antique that were she to acquire
   An eloquent mouth and tongue,
She would sit like an elder among the people, upright,
   And regale them with tales of ancient nations.
— A hand created for the pen or the sword
   "Struck" her [with water] in the mixing

Among elite and noble companions
  Who take their pleasures when they are within reach;
She then crawled through their limbs,
  Just as a medicine crawls through a sick man,
And had the effect upon the house when she was mixed
  That the morning has upon the night;
And the night traveler was guided by her
  Just as travelers are guided by markers and cairns.
      (D. iii, 269–71)

The poem hints strongly at (some of) the reasons for which wine poetry became a favorite register among later Sufi (mystical) poets.

Hakam is the tribe to which Abu Nuwas claimed to belong through his dead father's clientage rather than by blood. There is a faint evocation of a tribal context in the first line; essentially it is a brief "emotional prelude", since the motif of sleeplessness is particularly associated in the poetic tradition with the pains of love. This is a *nasib* reduced to a minimum and wine thus emerges as a balm to suffering. Wine displaces love; indeed, woven into the numinous ideal of an antique draught, there is an obviously erotic resonance to the piercing of the "virginal" wine. The imagery is highly paradoxical: wine is both hoary and ancient *and* a virginal maiden to whom youthful vigor returns once "she" is unsealed; in Arabic the feminine gender of the "daughter of the vine" is played up semantically. There is more to the image of the grey head scarf: in addition to the mature age of the wine, it is intended to conjure the physical picture of a wine vat covered over time with grey or white cobwebs. There is a tangible reality in this idealism.

The nobility of the boon companions, whose presence is almost entirely diminished by the wine which "regales" them, is succinctly expressed in the phrase "a hand created for the pen or the sword". The entourage of imbibers – their host certainly – is both learned and heroic. This is not quite the dry mock-heroism we find in so many other *khamriyyat*, but it is part of the same general tendency of transforming the old martial spirit of traditional, ancient poetry into values of comportment more appropriate to a "saturnalian" milieu.

Jonah Comes Out of the Whale

> "Th'hydroptic drunkard, and night-scouting thief,
> The itchy lecher, and self-tickling proud
> Have the remembrance of past joys, for relief
> Of coming ills ..."
>
> (John Donne, *Divine Meditations*)

There is a common and understandable view in Arabic literary history that Abu Nuwas repented of drinking wine, and of dissoluteness in general (*mujun*), before the end of his life. The idea is supported by several ascetic poems which seem to tell us as much. But the poems cannot be located in the chronology of the author's life; and as with most of his poetry one can only have a vague sense of when they were written. The ascetic poem may at times be an exercise in pious expression, perhaps commissioned by a patron. And devoutness may be a fleeting sentiment; it may have been sincere at any point in time but that was no guarantee of permanence. It is a standard motif in Arabic poetry that *tawba* (repentance) is a precarious thing. We have seen this in the dialogue with the Devil, which dramatized the (attempted) erosion of resolve in the most vivid way. The poet appeared to keep that resolve in tact, but the Devil's oath in the final line is a menacing threat and the poem ends in a tense ellipse ...

There are many declarations in Abu Nuwas's *khamriyyat* that move fervidly and consciously in a direction contrary to remorse: from piety into sin and decadence. The poet's posture is that he was pious as a youth and discovered self-indulgence subsequently:

> I bought depravity at a high price and sold
> Piety in return for a nice crop of pleasures. (*D.* iii, 98)

Two things governed the giving up of wine.

1. If we take religious piety temporarily out of the equation we are left with the calm propriety of old age and grey hair. In early Arabic poetry the lyric celebration of sundry indulgences is often set, according to a standard posture, firmly in the past. However vivid the scene depicted may be, in the putative present from which the poet looks back on his life the mantle of respectability has already been donned. Wine is a thing of the past. This is not religious repentance as such (it existed before Islam); it is the obligation of decency and forbearance (*hilm*) – the latter being perhaps *the* cardinal virtue inherited by Islamic society from the *Jahiliyya*. This ethos was understood and inherited by the later Islamic poets. Lyric celebration still often remained a nostalgic evocation of events set in the past.

2. In addition the later poets, from the early seventh century onward, also acquired the religious virtues of Islam. Repentance loomed large among them and so became a motif that capped the past posturing of hedonistic gratification. But not always; as al-Mutanabbi once said, "Is it wine that you repent of or its abandonment?"

The wine poetry of Abu Nuwas, and those of his ilk, is distinct from earlier poets in two ways. The first has been put eloquently by Hamori (1973: 71):

> [The early 'Abbasid *Khamriya*] is contrary to the archaic *nasib* in that the pre-Islamic poets used to recall a full past in a vague present, while the *khamriya* poet sees the party in the tavern as the very moment for which the wine has been stored since time immemorial: for him *now* is when the various predestined parts of the experience find one another.

We have already encountered this: "... *a wine [preserved] for the day when she is pierced*". There is no aftermath to this moment; the poem ends in a sort of mystical intoxication. The wine poem telescopes time into the short period of a Bacchic fling. But there are significant instances when the moment of indulgence is survived. In the seduction poems we have read

Abu Nuwas often has to face up to the brief recriminations of his waking victims – though he need not experience any self doubt; if he does, he mutters it under his breath. The following poem, however, is the most striking example of the poet stretching his celebration of indulgence to a point in time where he is forced to face up to remorse. This is a poem in which we sense that repentance was palatable because so eloquently contrived; it emerges exquisitely from both the structure and themes of this exceptional poem. It is a long and animated descriptive masterpiece, richly textured with Qur'anic (and Biblical) allusion and structured according to a sublime paradox whereby repentance emerges not simply as the natural end-point of a life of heedless comfort but also from the very elevated imagery with which wine is celebrated.

Five lines into the poem Abu Nuwas has arrived at a tavern on a tempestuous night:

> ... We roused the owners of the wine-shop
> In a night-cohort, turbulent and swollen,
>> Like the sea which dazes the sailor with fear.
> Suddenly at that moment there appeared a *heathen* crone,
>> Like a solemn anchoress,
> Tracing her lineage back through infidel stock,
>> Monastic idol-worshippers,
> Inquiring, "Who are you?" We replied, "People you know,
>> Every one open-handed, noted for his prodigality,
> Who, along the way, have stopped at your house: so seize
>> The liberality of the generous and name your price,
> For you have won a life of ease, provided you seize from us
>> What David seized from Goliath.
> Be lively in making a profit from them, doing – at the same
>> time –
>> A noble deed until they have left your house.
>> Then you can sleep like the dead!"
> She said, "I have what you want. Wait until morning."
>> We replied, "No, bring it now!"
> It is itself the morning; its clear radiance dispels
>> The night when it shoots out sparks like rubies

As the patrolling angels do, when, at night, they stone
　　With the stars the rebellious demon Afrits.
It advanced in the cup as bright as the sun at day-break,
　　Poured from an amphora upturned, bleeding at the waist.
We said to her, "How long has it been in the amphora,
　　Since it was hidden away?" She replied, "It was made in the
　　　　time of Saul.
It was concealed in the amphora and has grown to be
　　An old spinster buried inside a coffin in the earth.
It has been brought to you from the depths of its resting place,
　　So be careful not to take it in the cup with food."
The odor that wafts from it to the drinkers was like
　　The scent of crushed musk from a newly slit vesicle;
When mixed with clear rain-water
　　It was like a network of pearls on a ruby brocade
Carried round by [a youth] like the moon with large black eyes
　　From which the magic of Harut could have sprung.
With a lutenist in our midst who moves as he sings
　　"Abode of Hind in Dhat al-Jiz', Hail!"
...

Until when the sphere of the strings, together with the drums,
　　Spins us round, we are left as if in a trance.
We glorify in it in gardens thick with
　　Myrtle, acacia, pomegranate and mulberry,
Where the birds distract you from every other pleasure
　　When they warble in antiphonal strains.
Blessing be upon that time which slipped away too quickly –
　　A lovely time which was not hateful to me then.
Frivolity could not divert me from plunging into the midst of
　　　　[wine's] fray
　　And I did not fail to respond to its rallying cries
Until, lo! Grey hair surprised me by its appearance –
　　How hateful is the appearance of cursed grey hair
In the eyes of beautiful women; when they see its appearance,
　　They announce severance and separation from love.
Now I regret the mistakes I have made
　　And the misuse of the times prescribed for prayer.
I pray to you, God, praised be Your name!, forgive me

Just as You, Almighty One, forgave Him of the Fish (Jonah)!
(*D.* iii, 61–4)

In the final four lines we see the poet shaken from a narcotic trance by rejection. Exploring the contradiction that is built into this poem the present author has remarked elsewhere: "The final allusion to biblical Jonah, whom we realize at the end is evoked by the "tempestuous night", is enhanced by a handful of similar references interspersed throughout the poem: at line 7 the "heathen crone" is told to despoil the poet and his companions (i.e., to accept their money) "as David despoiled Goliath"; at line 10 sparks of wine are the stars hurled at rebellious demons by patrolling angels; at line 13 the amphora in which the wine is kept is said to date from the time of Saul, the King of Israel appointed by Samuel; in the following line the wine's storage in a coffin (*tabut*) makes allusion to the Ark of the Covenant (also *tabut*); in line 18 the Saqi is so bewitching as to be said to be the source of Harut's magic ("Harut" is an angel imprisoned in Babel with "Marut", where they teach sorcery). This chain of references is sealed with that of Jonah. Since rhyme is part of the signature of any poem, the significance of these references is accentuated by the fact that they provide the rhyme word of six lines (note: the sounds "-ut" and "-it" are considered to rhyme in Arabic): *Jalut* (Goliath), *Murrad al-'Afarit* (Rebellious demon Afrits), *Talut* (Saul), *Harut*, and *sahib al-Hut* ("He of the Fish" = Jonah). Each reference, less the final one, is part of an allegorical sequence that enhances the status of the wine. Yet the aura of hallowed bacchism thus affected is destroyed when a contradictory moral is conjured through the allusion to Jonah, who – we should remind ourselves – having obdurately resisted his divine calling was forced to recognize the will of God. In this manner the poem's essential antithesis is contrived through a redemption story that lies latent in the imagery – to the same degree as the events – of the narrative." (Kennedy, 1997, 235–6)

Abu Nuwas probably never gave up the desire to drink wine before his final sickness. But this poem allows us to think that he might have. We, in any case, will have cause to discuss the theme of wine a little further in reading some poems of praise. No genre of classical Arabic poetry is hermetically sealed off from the themes of all or any others.

"THE GOOD, THE BAD AND THE UGLY"

On Panegyric and Satire

THE PANEGYRIC

"Praise for al-Amin is honest and sincere;
  [But] there is much mendacious and dishonest praise" (D. i, 260)

Honesty and sincerity are at a premium in a genre of poetry
written for recompense. The panegyric (Ar. *madih*) is poetry in
praise of a patron, ruler or eminent person. By the late pre-
Islamic period when certain poets began to travel across the
Arabian peninsula and southern Iraq in search of patrons for
their eulogistic verse, it was associated with reward and remuneration. It is this fact that might have stymied ingenuousness.
Al-Fadl ibn Yahya ibn Khalid, brother of Ja'far the Barmecide,
remarked appropriately at some verses which Abu Nuwas
once wrote for him: "You have made me a pimp!" Money and
mediation were essential elements in this poetic milieu; and,
notwithstanding the fact that this remark was made in jest, it
does not mask totally the distaste that was deliberately evoked
and which the poet may have shared. In short, panegyric was
not, relatively speaking, Abu Nuwas's poetic bailiwick or *forte*.

Yet socially it was the most significant of the genres of poetry.
And, historically, we can encapsulate its significance by drawing
an arc between, on the one hand, the profuse poems composed
in honor of the prophet Muhammad in the Islamic late middle

ages, some of the most popular and widespread poems of their day (accounting for a relative majority of antique manuscripts of poetry), and, on the other hand, certain of the most famous poems from the early canon of Arabic literature, and especially the "Mantle" (*Burda*) poem of Ka'b ibn Zuhayr which was written for the Prophet; he rewarded Ka'b by conferring his mantle upon him. The Prophet Muhammad had his own court poet, the Medinan Hassan ibn Thabit who wrote largely in the mold of pre-Islamic tribal poets. Indeed, Hassan was, or had been, himself a "tribal poet" of the Ansari (i.e., Medinan convert) tribe of Khazraj. Extant pre-Islamic poetry is not anathema to Islam; it contains few pagan elements, which either means that there never had been many or that they were soon filtered out by Muslim posterity. It is quite striking, in fact, that monotheistic elements in pre-Islamic poetry outnumber pagan ones; they reflect the monotheistic milieu (Jewish, Christian, and, so-called, *hanif*) with which pre-Islamic paganism coexisted, though some were undoubtedly later interpolations.

Arab poets wrote in a traditional mold inherited from pre-Islamic Arabia, as discussed. It was a tradition that had developed significantly in the century before Islam (– the earliest poems survive from the early sixth century). Poets were also considered to "say that which they do not do", according to a famous Qur'anic characterization (26: 226); this is denigration, certainly, but by no means an outlawing of their practice. A combination, then, of poetic tradition and Islamic acceptance explains why the famous "Hamziyya" of Hassan ibn Thabit, which celebrated in panegyric mode the Prophet's conquest of Mecca in 630, contains in its prelude an idealized description of wine. It defies logic to consider these verses as inauthentic.

Though their language and rhetorical style changed greatly with time, panegyric poems from late pre-Islamic times well into the Abbasid era *tended* to be structured as follows:

1. An amatory prelude (Ar. *nasib*); this was written in nostalgic and elegiac mode; its principal motif was the

doleful description of the abandoned and time-worn
traces of the beloved's desert tribal encampment; the
poet introduces a sense of loss which the remainder of the
poem allows him to transcend and come to terms with;

2. A desert journey (Ar. *rahil*); this can be understood as
both a literal and structural move into the final
panegyric section: the poet describes a journey
(implicitly or explicitly to his patron) mounted on his
camel, to which animal he promptly turns his poetic
lens; this is to view the "*rahil*" as purely functional, when
in fact it contains elaborate and eloquent descriptions
(Ar. *wasf*) of the desert and its fauna, reflecting the
Bedouin origins of the whole tradition;

3. The panegyric section; the patron is praised as a paragon
of society's cardinal virtues, both Bedouin and Islamic:
generosity, bravery, forbearance, fidelity to the tribal
group, and, in the Islamic period, impeccable faith.

By the time of the great Abbasid panegyricists, Abu Tammam
(d. 845) and al-Buhturi (d. 897), the middle section had been
largely reduced and the poems became, according to the view
of modern scholarship, largely bi-partite (and even bi-polar)
rather than tri-partite. There are some exceptions that tend to
be stylized to meet a specific occasion such as Abu Nuwas's panegyric for al-Khasib, his benefactor in Egypt, in which the
poet's journey from Iraq across the Levant to Fustat is
described in "cartographic" detail. Most of Abu Nuwas's panegyrics are bi-partite rather than tri-partite; and some are simply occasional short pieces and fragments. He tended to reduce
the amatory *nasib* to a token minimum, where he included one
at all; in his bi-partite poems the prelude is often simply a celebration of wine. The panegyric materials of Abu Nuwas discussed below are divided into three sections: (A) Formal and
Sober; (B) Less Formal and Less Sober; and (C) Occasional and
Miscellaneous Eulogy.

* * * * *

A. Formal and Sober

Praise for Harun al-Rashid Abu Nuwas composed at least
five poems in honor of the tall, handsome, upright and dignified
potentate Harun al-Rashid, the caliph most associated in the
Arab and Muslim historical imagination with an Abbasid
Golden Age; the sovereign who, by the late middle ages of the
Arabian Nights, had become the symbol of a mythic and more
pristine past.

The poet was never properly accepted by al-Rashid, who
imprisoned him on at least one occasion, as we know. If Abu
Nuwas had been better received by the Barmecides while they
wielded extraordinary influence at the caliphal court before
803, the situation with al-Rashid might have been different. It
was, in any case, inevitable that Abu Nuwas would eulogize this
caliph intermittently whether he was in favor or not – indeed,
precisely to curry favor. The extant poems vary in tone and
quality (and length). One is a prison poem, from a fair number
that he composed during his life, pleading for the sovereign's
forgiveness, though never clarifying what offense he had com-
mitted. It appears to have been some kind of perceived treach-
ery: "I did not betray you behind your back" is all he says on the
subject. His life of indulgence would occasionally have exacerbated the effect of other misdemeanors. The essence of getting
on in society was to find favor with, and to avoid falling foul of,
the people in positions of influence; and if one patron was not
forthcoming others were there to be approached. They could
be played off against each other. Al-Fadl ibn Rabi', successor to
the enormous ministerial power of Yahya al-Barmaki, com-
pensated to some extent (eventually) for Abu Nuwas's lack of
success with the Barmecides; but it is noticeable that some of
the poet's spates in prison were due to the fact that he managed
to vex even al-Fadl. If it was politically expedient (for the sake
of the sovereign's reputation, for example, during the troubled
reign of al-Amin) al-Fadl could counsel on the "public relations" benefit of the decadent poet's incarceration.

A long panegyric for Harun was, according to one source, written on the advice of the Nawbakht family when he returned from Egypt – to appease the caliph upon re-emerging from an exile that had effectively been a flight from the sovereign's wrath. He received 20,000 dirhams in payment: rare compensation. (If one credits this account of the background of the poem in question one must reject the view that he only returned from Egypt after Harun's death in 809! Much of what we are told about Abu Nuwas is intrinsically contradictory.)

Another panegyric is remarkable since of its thirteen lines six are devoted to the description of wine; they dominate the prelude. The fact is surprising not because it does not make poetic sense but because of what we know of the venerable and sober public demeanor of the patron. The eminent grammarian and philologist al-Mubarrad (d. 898 or 899) later commented about this fact:

> "I know of no poet who has praised a caliph and composed such a prelude (nasib). However, he was serious in his praise and achieved his desired goal. Al-Rashid was protective of his dignity and shunned the mention of 'kisses' or 'wine' or any such things on account of his majesty and nobility; idle acts of decadence were anathema to him. However, Abu Nuwas was used to attaching to his majestic panegyric poems preludes which reflected his own situation and deportment." (D. i, 20)

There is an anecdote which relays the actual occasion when Abu Nuwas recited the poem to al-Rashid (an anecdote which both confuses this poem with the one which was composed upon Abu Nuwas's return from Egypt and brings the Barmecides, long disgraced at this point in history, back into the fold for the occasion).

> Al-Rashid would not listen to poetry that had distasteful or frivolous elements in it. So in the love poetry that was a prelude to praise for him no kisses or winks would be mentioned. When Abu Nuwas returned from Egypt, he wrote a panegyric and was received on the mediation of the Barmecides. He recited the

[poem beginning] 'I have long been crying at the traces of the abodes' and when he reached the description of wine al-Rashid's face changed; reciting the verse '*If wine has destroyed my inherited fortune ...*' Al-Rashid went quiet; when he recited

'*I drank a cup of wine that was like the lantern of the sky ...*'
He wanted to bring him to heel, but when he recited

'*God bless the one who has governed matters with power and competence ...*' he was moved and ordered him to be paid 20,000 dirhams. (*D.* i, 121)

In a rudimentary way this story provides insight into the psychology, or the perceived psychology according to medieval Arab poetics, of the multi-themed (bi-partite or tri-partite) panegyric poem. The first part was meant to stir the emotions, in an aesthetic and affective initial response to the poetry, so that the patron might be more receptive to the ensuing praise. The anecdote reflects this fundamental paradigm.

The finest poem in praise of Harun al-Rashid, according to the norms of the genre, is also one of the longest and most formal *qasida*s in the panegyric section. It gives us a glimpse of the fact that if Abu Nuwas was not a full-time professional panegyricist, like al-A'sha before him or Abu Tammam and al-Mutanabbi after him, it is because he lacked the temperament rather than the requisite poetic talent.

The poem is translated in full below. The rhyming consonant, the guttural "q", is relatively rare, difficult and majestic. The meter is the dignified *Kamil* (the "Perfect" or "Complete"). It is at once a poem giving thanks for release (from prison no doubt), a fact referred to in an early line but which apparently had taken place some time before composition, and also a polite but nevertheless quite direct plea for sustenance and recompense. The last line makes this amply clear and may appear abrupt and prosaic in this respect, referring to poetry effectively as marketable goods.

Prelude

Time has become ragged, though my ardor is still fresh,
    And I have fired an arrow targeting my youth;
But the arrow has fallen short of its goal,

Like a chaser kept behind stragglers;
My strengths have been diminished, I have become slow,
Though I once had vigor in supple joints.

* * *

Reminiscence of a Falcon Hunting
I would go out in the early morning with a glove for a
trained falcon,
A speedy catcher dressed in resonant bells,
A noble bird trained delicately
To capture its clumsy game;
Its carnelian eyes clear of impure flecks,
Its eyelids healthy and unstitched;*
Its new feathers like a cloak
Woven by the most skilled weaver,
Draped like a silk garment
Not quite covering the legs;
If you witnessed its contest when the cloud of dust
Fell away you would see it was noble and brave:
A goose was held in the beak of this bold
And hungry falcon, pulling at the flanks of its prey;
It had selected the largest and most sluggish,
Clasping it in long and sharpened claws.
Then we raised the cooking pot upon the fire
And the meat either fell apart from stewing
Or was cut up inside.

* * *

Adumbration of Full Panegyric
This is the Prince of the Faithful who rescued me
When my soul was between my larynx and throat.†
May I be [his] ransom for the day he [showed] me his favor;
If it were not for his sensibility and forbearance I would not
have been released;
You deemed my [blood] illicit to you though it was quite licit,
And you pulled [me] together when [I] had fallen apart;

* i.e., it was not captured in the wild which would have required it to
be hooded when kept domestically
† i.e. close to exiting the body through the mouth

The Camel Journey and the Oryx

So goad your mount on towards the court of a caliph,
    The first ever to attain his high goals;
We make our way to you from Sulayb and Jasim
    Across the highland at a quick and steady pace
Our camels follow an oryx cow which
    Gazes with the eyes of a mother bereft of her child ...
A flat-nosed beast looking for her calf upon soft ground
    With feelings of deranged intensity
And when she finds it, all she sees
    Is a hide torn and dragged [across the dust]

* * *

Fulsome Praise

Harun the Caliph disdains all but a pure essence
    That has taken strength in his very core;
A sovereign whose nature and temperament is decent:
    Sweet to the mouth of those who taste him;
He meets [and deals with] all matters of religious duties
    And takes care of the enemy that has him in his sights;
He protects you from actions he mulls over discreetly within
        himself
    With laughter and a bright face that spares you any doubt;
But when he has determined his opinion [of how to act]
    He grabs the very ears and mouth of his foe.
I swear to you the solemn oath of
    All those who trim and shave their hair [ritually after
        pilgrimage]:
You have shown fear and respect of God in perfect measure
    And striven above and beyond the striving of the pious;
You have sown fear among the polytheists so that
    Even their unformed semen fears you [long before birth]

* * *

The Petition

The goods of a poet are saleable when you deem them so
    And what you deem unsaleable remains unsold
        (D. i, 110–16)

To the untrained eye the poem may come across as a series of discrete and incongruously juxtaposed tableaux. Even so, there would be pleasure to be had from the depictions individually; we are innately moved by: the anxiety of fading youth; the exquisite beauty of a hunting falcon; the tragedy of a mother (an oryx cow) discovering her child (calf) butchered upon the ground; the charisma of a powerful and effective leader; and we can relate to the need for material sustenance. But in Arabic panegyric poetry there is also an unspoken dynamic working across such segments of a poem. Though this dynamic was an atavistic reflex of composition it also developed progressively from pre-Islamic to Abbasid times. There is a broad arc in this particular poem between the prelude and the culmination of the panegyric. Briefly (and simplistically), there is:

- — a movement from loss (fading youth, diminishing strength, the effects of Time) to gain (the victories and religious scruples of the caliph: the basis of a thriving society). This gain is meant both broadly in a historical context and pointedly (and with a touch of bathos) in the poet's final appeal for recompense;

- — a move from the past (reminiscence, youth) to a celebration of the present and future, symbolized in the person of the sovereign; related to this is

- — a progression from a sense of transcendent Time (the prelude) to transcendent Religion (Islam);

- — the success of the hunting falcon adumbrates the victories of the caliph; this section also undoubtedly reflects the "cynegetic" passion of the author and his patron;

- — the oryx section, far shorter than equivalent sections in pre-Islamic poetry, sustains the elegiac key of the poem's prelude; death is evoked solemnly before celebration of the death-dealing (and, by inference, life-giving) caliph; procreation is evoked obliquely in the remarkable image of future generations of fearful infidels.

The camel/journey section of this *qasida* is relatively short compared to the usual paradigm of the panegyric genre. Here the standard description of the feisty mount worn ragged by lengthy journeying has been both displaced by the detailed description of the hunt with the falcon and outshone by the beauty of the short but striking oryx tableau which medieval commentators noticed may have been inspired in particular by a line in Labid ibn Rabi'a's pre-Islamic *Mu'allaqa*. There is indeed an archaizing aspect to this poem in the description of fauna; for all that Abu Nuwas was a quintessential "Modern" poet in his lyric verse his hunting poems and descriptions of fauna in general show that he was still highly partial to the difficult specialized lexicon which is associated with the more archaic desert poetry. (His so-called *Manhuka* [because of its "truncated" verses] dedicated to al-Fadl ibn Rabi'a is an epitome of this mode. It describes a journey made to his patron, taking advantage of this fact to describe fauna, notably the desert onager, in extraordinary detail. The poem had a whole commentary devoted to it by Ibn Jinni in the tenth century.)

There is an amusing anecdote about the penultimate line, concerning the propriety of describing matters of life and death as if wrested from God's control:

> ... Kulthum ibn 'Amr al-'Attabi met Abu Nuwas and said to him, "Are you not ashamed before God for having written,
>
> ' *You have sown fear among the polytheists so that*
>
> *Even their unformed semen fears you [long before birth].'* "

Abu Nuwas retorted, "And you!? Were you not wary of God when you wrote,

> ' *... You have continued to strive kindly for me*
>
> *So that I have snaffled death from the hands of my demise.'* "

Al-'Attabi responded, "...You have a ready answer for all who would advise you!"

B. Less Formal and Less Sober

For al-'Abbas ibn 'Abdallah Al-'Abbas ibn 'Abdallah, also know as al-'Abbas ibn Ja'far, was the grandson of Abu Ja'far al-Mansur (d. 775), the second Abbasid caliph. Little is written about the relationship between poet and patron. As an Abbasid prince al-'Abbas was socially eminent by definition; on the evidence of the number of poems dedicated to him, and the relatively informal tone which they adopt, he and Abu Nuwas appear to have been quite close.

Abu Nuwas accompanied al-'Abbas on pilgrimage to Mecca one year and composed this poem to celebrate his patron's charity on the occasion. The poet's motives were mixed, though. He was loath to admit his own indigence, yet he was taking advantage of the fact that his patron had loosened his purse strings.

The abodes of Nawar! Why have the abodes of Nawar
    Cloaked you in sorrows, blithe though they are themselves?

* * *

They say that grey hair brings dignity to its people;
    My grey hair, thank God, does no such thing!
For I have not desisted from receiving the favors
    Of a faun who strives around with the cup of wine;
A fresh wine like carnelian when mixed with water
    For which men have bargained hard at the merchant's stall;
It is as if the remnants of bubbles disappearing on its surface
    Are scattered hints of grey upon the black down of a cheek;
The wine was cloaked in cobwebs until they were rent from its
        skin
    Just as the night is torn away from the day;
The palm which hands you this wine has fingers
    Which meet the eye like the row of teeth on a comb.

* * *

I have now sworn a devout oath unmixed with
    Decadence – I could never swear a decadent oath;

Al-'Abbas made people's pilgrimage one of rectitude;
   He managed it with asceticism and dignity;
He guided them through the waymarks of their religion and
     showed them
   The torch lamps of rectitude, one after the other;
He gave food to the hungry all the way to Mecca
   And distributed gifts without ever stalling or postponing;
And you could see the pilgrims who had set out on shank's mare
   Carried upon his mounts, caravan upon caravan [all the way to
     Mecca];
O 'Abbas, your charitable soul and noble origin
   Made you reject the bejeweled ornaments of this world;
You descend from al-Mansur, the "Victorious One" of Banu
   Hashim,
   After whom one's pride can have no [other];
Your two grandparents were the best of Qahtan, on the one
   hand,
   And considered the best of Nizar, on the other.
I was brought to you by a need I have not disclosed;
   I hide it away for fear of gloaters,
So drape over me the veil of your kindness
   With which you covered my defects in the past.
     (*D*. i, 148–50)

"Nawar" in the opening verse is a symbolic name for the archetypical beloved of the *nasib*; Labid ibn Rabi'a addressed a departed "Nawar" in his pre-Islamic *Mu 'allaqa*; in Abbasid times the impersonal resonances of the name would have been obvious. This is a token and dismissive *nasib*.

Al-Mansur, the patron's grandfather, was the second Abbasid caliph and founder of Baghdad in 762–3. Abu Nuwas puns on the meaning of this name, the "Victorious". The patron's grandparents are made to represent the two great divisions of Arab tribes, the Northern Arabians (here represented by Nizar) and the Southern Arabians (Qahtan).

This poem is particularly notable for its ethical transition from the bacchic section to eulogy proper. The poet at first pretends to eschew sobriety and dignity even after his hair has turned grey but he then countermands this posture in the line that leads into the formal *madih*. Each register of celebration has its own norms: first waggish bacchism then praise of an Abbasid prince performing the Hajj and who has therefore forsworn the pleasures which he formerly enjoyed. Celebration of piety thus benefits from the contrast with dalliance. This is a generous patron and former drinking companion performing his religious duties properly.

It is significant that this poem was apparently known to Harun al-Rashid. His reaction is very telling as to the kind of reception we might expect this poem to have had in conservative society. It is related that

> … when Harun al-Rashid heard this poem he disliked the line "… *grey hair brings dignity to its people; my grey hair, thank God, does no such thing!*"
>
> He said to al-Fadl [ibn Rabi'], "Tell this reprobate [*majin*], 'Do you deny that grey hair brings dignity when God's messenger himself, peace be upon him, said, "No believer ever turns grey without this providing a veil that protects him from the Fire"?' "
>
> Al-Fadl summoned the poet and told him. He replied, "I did not deny that dignity comes with grey hair or the contents of the prophetic tradition; however, my *own* grey hair has not brought with it dignity given the way I hasten towards sins and put off repentance. The following line bears witness to the fact: '*I do not desist from receiving the favors of a fawn*'."
>
> Al-Fadl told this to al-Rashid who laughed and replied, "He knows best his own inner self and the unsightliness of his acts!"

So, it is not the fact of celebrating wine and decadence generally, or of juxtaposing wine and decadence with the celebration of the piety of the Hajj, that is deemed unseemly, but the apparent contradiction of a particular detail from prophetic tradition. It was not then the contents of poetry itself which necessarily dictated a poet's success in society but the (to some extent random) reaction of those in positions of power and patronage.

A number of poems written for al-Amin are constructed according to this basic paradigm: a section of bacchic lyricism is followed by (at times perfunctory) praise. The more unique poems written for the pleasure-loving al-Amin were those which celebrated his luxurious riverboats shaped variously as a lion, an eagle and a dolphin.

C. Occasional and Miscellaneous Eulogy

The Debate between Munificence and Beauty "Debate literature" (Ar. *munazara*) in the medieval Arabic canon became established from the ninth century onwards. It was essentially a prose literature with a heritage going back to the tribal contests (*munafara*s and *mufakhara*s) of the pre-Islamic and early Islamic periods. In the ninth century al-Jahiz wrote a number of debates which can be considered the progenitor of the prose genre in its developed Arabic form (– which is not an Arab invention since "The genre was practiced in the Middle East in Sumerian, Akkadian, Persian and Syriac before it appeared in Arabic"; cf. *EAL*). One of these debates of al-Jahiz is particularly significant: "His 'Contest of Winter and Summer', which is lost, may have been a 'true' literary debate *where the concepts themselves are the antagonists.* The earliest surviving true debates date from the eleventh century." Abu Nuwas of course flourished a few decades before al-Jahiz and in the following charming fragment we find a "true" debate in miniature that dates from even earlier than the lost "Contest of Winter and Summer". The poem is in praise of a certain Ibrahim al-'Adawi.

> Munificence and Beauty quarreled over you
>> And began to debate
> The former said, 'His right hand is mine
>> For charity, benevolence and giving.'
> The latter replied, 'His face is mine
>> For handsomeness, elegance and perfection.'
> They then separated, pleased with each other,
>> Each one having spoken the truth. (*D.* i, 297)

The Prison Guard Among the twenty-four poems listed in the
Diwan as "panegyrics composed by the poet when he was
detained", there is one that seems to fit the category of eulogy
only by a feat of mental agility. The fact is that it is simply
grouped together with other materials written to or for a
patron. "He wrote to al-Fadl ibn al-Rabi' through Bakr ibn
al-Mu'tamir complaining about his prison guard who was
called Sa'id":

> May I be your protection from death! – add more chains to me!
>> Double my dose of the lash and the club!
> Appoint as sentry over me and the doors
>> Of my cell every rebellious devil
> And give my ears reprieve from the filthy,
>> Harsh voice of a man called Sa'id:
> He has left my chains feeling light
>> But his hatred [of me] has placed irons on my heart! (D. i, 244)

If this piece were placed among the homoerotic poems there
would be little cause to object.

"Hasan of Basra" Hasan of Basra, that is, Abu Nuwas, wrote
to al-Fadl ibn al-Rabi' from prison testifying solemnly to his
new ascetic demeanor. But that he – Abu Nuwas – was trying to
pass himself off as "Hasan of Basra", the legendary ascetic,
shows that he had not lost his sense of irony while incarcerated.

> You, Ibn al-Rabi', have taught me devoutness
>> And accustomed me to rectitude;
> My vanity has thus ceased, my ignorance abated –
>> I have exchanged them for chastity and asceticism;
> If you saw me now you would think of the virtuous Hasan of
>> Basra
>> Or the religious scholar Qatada;
> My humility is adorned with emaciation
>> And a locust-like jaundice.
> ...
> Pray for me ...
> And you will see a mark on my face from prayer

Which one is convinced is the result of worship;
If hypocrites were to see it one day
    They would want to buy it, deeming it ample testimony to
        their faith. (*D.* i, 246–7)

The sentiments of the last image in particular are conscious at some level of words that began this discussion of panegyric: "*There is much mendacious and dishonest praise* ..." – if this is praise.

* * * * *

"PENS DIPPED IN BITTER GALL": SATIRE

"*Born to no other but thy own disgrace,*
Thou art a thing so wretched and so base
Thou canst not ev'n offend, but with thy face;
And dost at once a sad example prove
Of harmless malice, and of hopeless love,
All pride and ugliness! Oh, how we loathe
A nauseous creature so composed of both! ..."

        (Rochester on Sir Carr Scroope)

"*Rail on poor feeble scribbler, speak of me*
In as bad terms as the world speaks of thee.
Sit swelling in thy hole like a vexed toad,
And full of pox and malice, spit abroad.
Thou canst blast no man's face with thy ill word:
Thy pen is full as harmless as thy sword."

        (Scroope on Rochester)

"*If that son of a bitch thinks he is safe from me*
   ...Well, I have unfurled my tongue
So that comparison be made between us in literary salons
   — So that his satire be measured with mine"

        (Abu Nuwas, *D.* ii, 119)

These last menacing lines were written about one "Zunbur", a jilted or jilting lover. Poets in medieval Islamic society known for their satirical talent were feared. The sting of satire (*hija'*) lasted for ever, as much of the poetry handed down to posterity corroborates. In a culture where fame was nothing if it was not also posthumous, the stigma of lampoon was to be avoided, and it would seem that the only antidote once it was received was for the victim to give as good as s/he got. Hence the numerous exchanges of satire (Ar. *naqa'id*) that are such a distinctive feature of early Arabic literature. In the *Diwan* of Abu Nuwas the *naqa'id* (sing. *naqida*) are categorized separately from the chapter of *hija'*; but the only real distinction between a poem of *hija'* and a *naqida* is that the latter is only one half of a satirical duel. (*Naqa'id* tend to come in pairs, having the same meter and sharing much in the way of vocabulary and imagery.)

Most amateurs of Arabic literature are familiar with the image, struck in an Umayyad *naqida*, of a mother urinating in full view of others to put out the hearth-fire whenever strangers approached. Generosity and hospitality were cardinal virtues, as was a proper sense of corporal dignity and shame. But here honor and self-respect are sacrificed to avarice. The image is an invention of vicious satire and was directed by al-Akhtal against his contemporary Jarir – they were two of the greatest and most respected of Umayyad poets. (Their lexically difficult *naqa'id* were commented on by Abu 'Ubayda, of the mosque-pillar incident, and remain one of the chief sources of the *Ayyam al-'Arab*, that is, accounts of battles and feuds between the pre-Islamic Arab tribes that constitute one of the earliest extant Arab histories.)

Yet compared to some of what ensues in this section the unsightly image of this avidly protective mother is relatively tame. The point about satire is (or could often be) that there was no incentive to pull punches. *Hija'* could certainly work well rhetorically with sustained linguistic invention (as in al-Mutababbi's famous satire of the Ikhshidid ruler of Egypt, Kafur); but it could also be the vulgar pugilist's equivalent of lining his gloves with horseshoes. And when *hija'* was not hideously obscene, it could be sexist, racist, scatological or religiously profane.

In the *Diwan* eight categories of *hija'* are identified, which include:

- — ten poems written "against the Bedou Arab tribes and the Basrans"; it was in one of these that he mocked the "Northern" tribes, who were politically dominant, vaunted the "Southern" tribes of "Qahtan" and managed to offend Harun al-Rashid so much that he was eventually imprisoned for his efforts;

- — twenty-five poems against the rulers and elite of society;

- — thirteen poems against religious scholars, philosophers and philologists etc.;

- — twenty-three poems against his peers (in addition to his *naqa'id* which were by definition directed against other poets);

- — a penultimate sub-category of twenty-five satires are labeled "excessively foul", an extraordinary qualification since there is much that accords with this register of satire in earlier classifications.

There was subtlety also in this apparently indelicate craft; and some lighthearted ribbing, as in the following fragment about a certain tightfisted Sa'id:

Bread and Bereavement

Sa'id's loaf of bread is worth as much to him as his soul;
   He kisses it sometimes, other times he plays with it,
He puts it on his lap and sniffs it,
   He holds it out before him and talks to it;
And when a poor man approaches him for it
   He would seem to have lost his mother and relatives!
     (*D.* ii, 151)

There are many anecdotes reminiscent of this sketch in al-Jahiz's *Book of Misers*, especially in the chapter about the (then) notoriously miserly people of Merv. A son once outdid his father's meanness with unusual inventiveness: the father had preserved a slab of cheese for ages by limiting guests to scraping their bread along its surface; when the son inherited the cheese upon the father's death he was even more careful, allowing his "guests" to flavor their bread only by waving it from above.

When Abu Nuwas, for his part, went on repeatedly about the cooking pots of his antagonist Fadl al-Raqashi being pristine white rather than blackened with soot, he was accusing him (in a standard image) of never cooking and certainly, therefore, of never being the generous host at a feast.

The Politics of State and al-Amin

Abu Nuwas may have been fairly indolent when it came to politics – perhaps wisely given the umbrage he provoked in other ways. However, the following lampoon of al-Amin and two of the sovereign's advisers shows the poet, on a rare occasion, taking exception to what he saw as political suicide on the part of his patron. In 810 the caliph appointed his son as his successor and named him "al-Natiq bi-l-Haqq". Abu Nuwas considered that al-Fadl ibn al-Rabi' (his own patron) and Bakr ibn al-Mu'tamir, as minister and counsel to the sovereign respectively, were responsible for the decision which could only enrage the caliph's powerful half brother, al-Ma'mun. With historical hindsight we notice dark presentiment in this poem; it has a grave undertone, notwithstanding the central passage of smuttiness that characterizes this kind of satire.

> The folly of the Imam has lost the caliphate,
>> That and the ignorance of his minister and incompetence of
>> his counselor;
> For Fadl, the Vizier, and Bakr, the counselor,
>> Are eager for something in which lies our Emir's ruin.
> This is all just reckless delusion –
>> The worst possible path to take!

* * *

Now, the Caliph's sodomy is strange
　　But stranger still is the Vizier's passive role,
For the latter is trodden upon while the former one treads –
　　A good example, by my life, of how things in general vary!
If the two of them were to leave each other alone
　　It would be a fine and honorable thing.
However, [the Caliph] is obsessed with Kawthar
　　Who will not desist from being impaled upon pricks;
Their behavior is deemed vile and back to front,
Like the pissing of a camel*

* * *

But I find even stranger than this, despite myself,
　　The appointment of a small child as successor –
One who cannot even wipe his own ass and who is
　　Scarcely out of the arms of his wet-nurse;
This is all down to Fadl and Bakr ...
O Lord! Take them both away swiftly
　　And place them in Hell's most torturous fire! (D. ii, 114–15)

Kawthar, the river of paradise, was the name of a eunuch with whom al-Amin was infatuated. *Imam,* here in the sense of "spiritual leader", and *Emir* both refer to the Caliph; *emir* means "prince" and stands for "Prince of the Faithful".

(*Note.* The attribution of this poem is, in fact, by no means certain: it is also attributed variously to Yusuf ibn Muhammad and 'Ali ibn Abi Talib (not the caliph of that name) in the historical works of Tabari (d. 923), Mas'udi (d. 956) and al-Jahshiyari (d. 942–3)).

Spite and Sacrilege

Malevolence towards Aban al-Lahiqi, his greatest literary nemesis, drove Abu Nuwas to write a poem associating him with dangerous sacrilege. It is from this poem, as much as any

---

* A proverbial saying, alluding to the fact that camels urinate backwards

other, that we have a clear picture of the overlap in the generic categories of *hija'* and *mujun*. The poem is so reckless that it contains a glaring grammatical mistake for which even a schoolboy would be severely reprimanded. Some anomalies in Abu Nuwas's Arabic are colloquial reflexes. In this case the very opposite is true: the author was passing off a mistake as naïve hyper-correction and placing it in the mouth of his adversary as part of his ridicule.

> I witnessed Aban one day
>   — May he not thrive! —
> When we were present in the
>   Emir's tent in Nahrawan;
> It was time
>   For the dawn prayer,
> So the Muezzin stood
>   To announce God's grace,
> Summoning the people to it
>   With elegant clarity —
> We repeated everything he said
>   Until the end of the Adhan.
> [Aban] asked us, "How can you give testimony
>   To all this, sight unseen?
> I will never give testimony
>   Except to what my eyes have born witness!"
> I said, "Praised be the Lord!"
>   He replied, "Praised be Mani!"
> I said, "Jesus is a Messenger!"
>   He replied, "— From Satan!"*
> I said, "Moses is the confidant
>   Of our Sovereign Giver of Blessing!"
> He replied, "Your Lord ... with

---

*   ... In a note Vincent Monteil wrote (*Abu Nuwas*, 1979, p. 186) "This poem shows that he had only a vague idea about this dualist religion. ... The Manicheans held Jesus in very high esteem. The mistake made by Abu Nuwas here stems no doubt from a confused notion held by some who thought that 'Jesus, crucified by the Jews, became the Devil in reality.'"

Eyes and ears!?*
Did he create Himself?
    Or who else, then!?" – I got up and abandoned
This heathen, draped in the clothes
    Of unbelief, to deny the Merciful One;
I stood and dragged off my robes
    Away from one who mocks the Qur'an;
Who wants to be an equal
    Of that band of libertines ('usbat al-mujjan):
Hammad al-'Ajrad, 'Ubad ibn Furat,
    Waliba ibn al-Hubab and
Muti' ibn Iyas –
    Who lamented the Twin Palms of Hulwan –
And 'Ali ibn al-Khalil,
    "The Boon Companions' Basil Stick".
But you and I are fornicators, both –
    Born of philanderers and loose women. (D. ii, 78–9)

Abu Nuwas was tarring Aban al-Lahiqi with the brush of Manichaean heresy (zandaqa). A few decades earlier this might have been more hazardous, as a campaign had been organized against heretics in the time of al-Mahdi (d. 775). There are indeed reports that Abu Nuwas was himself accused of, and imprisoned for, zandaqa on account of utterances less outrageous than the profanity above.

We have encountered some of the names listed at the end of the poem before, notably Abu Nuwas's tutor, Waliba ibn al-Hubab. They are the (in)famous "dissolutes of Kufa" by whom Abu Nuwas was enormously influenced. He was their principal successor in the Abbasid capital, and it would have been transparent to Abu Nuwas's audience that he was in fact much more connected with these "mujjan" than Aban.

---

* Aban's contempt for divine anthropomorphism, in the image evoked of Moses speaking to God, is undermined by the glaring solecism in "ears" which is in the Arabic nominative case when, according to the grammatical construction used, it should be in the genitive.

Tasteless Ja'far the Barmecide

How scarce elegant taste is among the people,
  Though they are like grains in a gravel pile,
With the exception of one man with whom the road brought me
    together
  As we traveled of a morning to al-'Askar;
He said, surmising that I was a poet,
  Just as I had surmised his sagacity (not knowing who he was),
"Will you not recite to me some of the poetry you have
    composed?
  Be sure not to omit the best and most majestic of it all."
So I recited poems in praise of the Barmecide
  Abu al-Fadl, that is, the young Ja'far.
And I was delighted by [my companion's] show of good taste, for
    he said,
  "Your poetry is like pearls. Were you rewarded with pearls?"
To which I replied in the manner of a poet
  Seeking to explain [being overlooked],
"If I praise a man made of shit
  Then I am rewarded too with shit!" (*D*. ii, 115–16)

Abu Nuwas had cast his eulogistic pearls at swine, so he claimed. We have discussed Abu Nuwas's relationship with the Barmecide family in Chapter 1. From among the eminent father (Yahya ibn Khalid) and his various sons, Ja'far ibn Yahya – renowned in his day for his learning and elegance until brutally executed by Harun al-Rashid in 803 – was the most detested by Abu Nuwas. It was Ja'far's indifference to his poetry which appears to have provoked this resentment, albeit the jealousy of Aban al-Lahiqi, the Barmecide stooge, seems to have been responsible for kindling the antipathy at the outset.

(Abu Nuwas in fact lamented the Barmecides after their tragic downfall. The poet Di'bil ibn 'Ali told of how he once stood with Abu Nuwas at the foot of Ja'far's jibbeted corpse; Di'bil assumed his friend would be content, given the way he had satirized the Barmecides so bitterly, but he simply said, "I did not desire this, even though I did say these things."

(D. ii, 51–2) By contrast, in a fit of resentment against al-Fadl ibn al-Rabi' the incarcerated Abu Nuwas cursed: "I wish to see you like Ja'far – your two halves divided [and exposed] upon a bridge.")

The Alchemist and Phony Genealogies

In a detailed lampoon of al-Haytham ibn 'Adi, the Abbasid genealogist, Abu Nuwas managed to pour scorn on not one but two professions:

> Even though you can, [as it were], change willow's wood to hard
>> For all those in search of [good] lineage,
> Those alchemists, despite exhausting themselves
>> With their efforts, are fruitless –
> They will never, however much they toil,
>> Make gold except from gold! (D. ii, 56–7)

Alchemy gets a bad press in its very principle. Genealogy, by contrast, was a genuine science; but it was liable to the abuse of Abbasid social climbers who forged specious lineages for themselves. Ashja' al-Sulami, a panegyricist of Harun al-Rashid and protégé of Ja'far the Barmecide, had a genealogy that was fabricated for him by his adopted tribe of Qays (among whom he was brought up as an orphan in Basra). Abu Nuwas scoffed at them all for this falsified ancestry: "They have made their ancestors into fornicators, yet if I had done the same they would have been incensed ... At home they have one lineage and another in public, like an old lady who wears a veil then reveals her ugly face."

Isma'il ibn Abi Sahl

The circumstances which led Abu Nuwas to lampoon some of his closest patrons are not always (properly) explained, nor are we given clues that allow us to place the poems within the various chronologies of the relationships he had. The background to these poems can be as enigmatic as the poems themselves were brutal. They are more than simply coarse banter, and some harsh motives or distasteful facts (or *perceptions* of fact) must often lie behind them. Satire was not just a nasty habit; unfortunately, when we are ignorant of the circumstances which provoked attack, it can often seem that it was. When his feelings for an individual were poisoned – for (no) good reason – he would often tarnish the image of that person's family. Sisters and mothers might be presented in sexually explicit scenes, with details elaborated about sexual preference and the various positions adopted. In this vein he accused Isma'il ibn Abi Sahl of an illicit relationship with his nephew:

> You made the illicit permissible with your sister's son
>> Then claimed, "I saw our elders do this."
> And you never screwed a mother's son
>> Without taking the mother first. (*D*. ii, 131)

Isma'il's brother, al-Fadl ibn Abi Sahl, was lampooned for siring twin girls. The fact was blamed graphically on the excessive and restless sex he had had when he sired the children – a feature ascribed to his Bactrian origins and a certain kinship with the camels of this region (which have two humps).

The Stolen Member

Sexual lampoons can be as farcical as they are religiously profane. Indeed, the following is as much preposterous fantasy as ridicule of a certain Abu Riyah.

> If you ever sleep next to Abu Riyah
>> Then sleep with your hand on your sword,
> For he has some women who,
>> In the evening, steal the tips of lances;
> Once, when I slept with him, they stole my penis
>> Which I only retrieved in the morning;
> It came back all scratched along the sides,
>> Moaning to me of its wounds ... (*D*. ii, 131)

The very next verse is an obscene distortion of the morning call to prayer placed in the mouths of "Abu Riyah's lascivious women".

Quack Philosopher of Egypt

While Abu Nuwas sojourned in Egypt the philosopher Hashim ibn Hudayj made the mistake of disparaging him. The poet's answer in verse – and withering sarcasm – was to depict him as not just a spurious philosopher but a quack sexual doctor to boot.

> All of us, Ibn Hudayj
>> Are slaves to your learning;
> However, medicine is the most worthy
>> Occupation for you.
> You are a veritable philosopher of this subject –
>> Perspicacious about the causes of infirmity.
> So why is it that the penis is light
>> But heavier when it stands?
> And when it empties its
>> Contents it wilts and hangs?
> Is this a contingent thing,
>> Or pre-eternal – sempiternal?
> And why is it pleasurable to rub
>> When this is done repeatedly,
> Yet when the pleasure is spent
>> The penis stoops over with fatigue? (D. ii, 110–111)

These kinds of impish physiological questions and answers (though the answers are naturally omitted) are to be found in other medieval texts. A good example is in the eleventh-century picaresque narrative by Ibn Butlan, *The Physicians' Cenacle*.

Onanist Job

Abu Nuwas satirized one Ayyub (Job) ibn Muhammad the Secretary (*Katib*):

> I have seen that true lovers when tormented
>> Seek comfort in tears and weeping.

Ayyub, however, when his heart recalls
  The one whose name we will not divulge, takes action:
He calls for an inkstand with a cotton ink-wad,
  Writes his [sweetheart's] name on his palm and masturbates.
If lovers were contented with what
  Contents you, no lovelorn person would ever complain.
    (D. ii, 98)

A Prison Consultation

Similarly, he satirized one Khamis with whom he was once imprisoned. He overheard Khamis consulting a Jurist Sheikh and fellow inmate about masturbation, and wrote the following spoof:

If you are to marry off a noblewoman to her equal
  Then marry Khamis to Palm daughter of Forearm;
Say: "You will gain a fine match by marrying a noblewoman
  Whose yard is spacious and surrounded by five children."
She is chaste when imprisoned
  And bound by heavy irons,
But if the fates ever manage [her] release
  He will have in her a substitute for every buxom maiden.
    (D. ii, 98)

The poem is inspired by a simple pun, for Khamis is formed from the root for "five" in Arabic – the fingers on a hand. The image of the "imprisoned", i.e. clenched, fist is apposite to the circumstances of composition. So supremely apposite that one suspects the poem gave rise to the anecdote.

Servants and Singing Girls

His way of mocking the effeminate "Zunbur" was to threaten to divorce him like a woman. He himself was accused of being effeminate; both Janan and 'Inan apostrophized him this way. Yet when one 'Ala' ibn al-Waddah called him "*ya mukhannath*" at the court of Yahya ibn Khalid the Barmecide, the man only succeeded in provoking a lampoon upon his own daughter, "who has lovers as [numerous as the striking of] *tabla*s on Palm Sunday".

He frequently mocked the singing-girls Barsum, Nabat and 'Inan, of whom he was doubtlessly fond, in extraordinarily burlesque hyperbole. Barsum's voice gave him a dose of small-pox; she had the aspect of an animal-bell in the palm of a leper (!?); and made him hoot at night with the owl, farting with love so hard as to wake up the distant Byzantine king. This is *hija'* as the anti-ideal of *ghazal*. For her part, Nabat's step was so large it could take her from Sheba to China; her face was like the new moon (invisible); her neck had the dimensions of an enormous snake; her smile was like a sick man's bowl; and she had a look in her eyes like the glint of a madman ... etc., etc.

But one – unnamed – *qayna* is derided with a finer conceit:

She demonstrates piety outwardly to God's people
   Then meets me with coquetry and a smile.
I went to her heart to complain [about her]
   But wasn't alone – there was a queue for a mile. (*D*. ii, 83)

Like so much, this is abstract, somewhat inflated metaphor. Yet some of the most interesting images are those that depict relatively innocuous personal details. He made fun of his beloved Janan, either during or after their relationship, describing how she pronounced her "j"-s as "z"-s: one day he heard her say "*zanaza*" for "*janaza*" ("funeral"). This is not particularly insulting, and seems simply to be the endearing detail of what he actually heard her say.

Fatal Provocation?

It is not hard to credit the belief that Abu Nuwas may have provoked his own demise with some unpalatable glibness. The version of his death according to which he was poisoned by the Nawbakht family is explained in one source with a brief chain of causes. He so offended "Zunbur" ("the louse hunter") with grotesque insults that in a fit of pique Zunbur falsely attributed some anti-Shi'ite verses to him and showed them to the Shi'ite Nawbakhtis. They secreted poison in his food which killed him after a period of four months – they had, in any case, apparently harbored resentment of their own against the poet ever since his acid ridicule of Isma'il ibn Abi Sahl and his mother Razzin.

But in the end one must be wary of the reflex of assuming that people are forever offended by invective directed against them. Charles II forgave an astonishingly vulgar indiscretion from Rochester who had placed a "terrible lampoon" in the monarch's hand (by mistake):

> ... Poor prince! thy prick, like thy buffoons at Court,
> Will govern thee because it makes thee sport.
> 'Tis sure the sauciest prick that e'er did swive.
> The proudest, peremptoriest prick alive ...

4

SOME HUNTING POEMS
AND A GAME OF POLO

"A hound like a flash of lightning, throwing up white stones, as he
gathers up the ground like something fried flying out of the pan"
(trans. Rex Smith)

Abu Nuwas hunted game and sang of the fact in extraordinary
descriptive poems. If he had written none of the other poetry
for which he was (and remains) either famed or notorious, he
would still occupy an important place in Arabic literary history
as the "supreme cynegetic poet" (*EAL*, art. "Tardiyya", J.E.
Montgomery). He represents the apogee of this genre in the
same way he does for the wine poem. The hunting poems probably date in bulk from his life in the Abbasid capital and owe
much in particular to the patronage and shared passion of
al-Amin; they may thus be a relatively late development in his
poetic endeavor. Though he begins one poem with the words,
"Hunting ... was my pleasure as a young man", this nostalgic
posture is something of a topos and one must be wary about
using the line as evidence in fixing a biographical scheme. We
can say with certainty that Abu Nuwas was as fond of the chase
as he was of wine, and on occasion he even placed these pleasures side by side in his verse:

"Oft I go forth early before morning is clear and before the slowly
advancing hens cluck, / With a [peregrine] ruddy and whitish in colour,
sitting up on the fist like a little eagle. / With garments tucked up away
from her feet, which seem to have been dyed with indigo ... My

companions continue with their dolce vita, eating the meat of their
quarry or drinking wine..." (trans. Rex Smith)

The hunting poem (Ar. *tardiyya*) was written largely in a special meter known as *rajaz*. It was an informal meter, eschewed
almost totally in other genres in which it was considered infer-
ior or substandard. A poem written in *rajaz* is known as an
urjuza, which also has some other formal features that need not
be described here. It was a meter of extemporization, which is
relevant as it seems there was, already in the Umayyad period,
a "practice of composing such pieces at the end of a hunt" (*EAL*).
Twenty-nine hunting *urjuzas* in Abu Nuwas's *Diwan* carry the
sterling-stamp of authenticity together with four *qasidas* (in
formal meter), and a substantial number of other hunting
poems are also attributed to him. It is the same situation as for
his love and wine poetry, i.e., the genres in which he excelled;
and as with much in those other genres, the persona detectable
in the more doubtful ascriptions is barely distinguishable from
the authentic core. Some special curios have been placed
among the "cynegetic" poems, notably, a poem describing a
polo match in Isabadh – a delightful piece conveying the energy
of the contest, apparently extemporized while players
indulged themselves with food and drink after a game.

Hunting poetry has a literary genealogy that goes back in
some form to pre-Islamic poetry; in this earlier canon

> ... hunting scenes are included within the polythematic *qasida*
> and are of two types; the professional, or 'primitive' hunt, and
> the aristocratic, or royal, hunt ... The professional hunt occurs as
> part of the camel description ..., the prey being the oryx and the
> wild ass ... The aristocratic hunt is linked with the personal vaunt
> and often concludes the ode: it is sometimes linked with equine
> description. (*EAL*)

Independent hunting poems are first attested in the poetic
remains of the Umayyad Abu al-Najm al-'Ijli (eighth century).
Abu Nuwas was thus part of a lineage that preceded him and
extended beyond him to the end of the tenth century and, to a

limited extent, thereafter (there survives, for example, a hunting *urjuza muzdawija*, i.e. in rhyming couplets, by Ibn Nubata from the fourteenth century). In the later period some changes in diction can be seen, but the genre also then came, essentially, to a fairly abrupt halt. Abu Nuwas's

> ... *tardiyyat* are crisp and vivid metonymical descriptions of the chase and can be categorized as (a) the early morning expedition (the prototype of which is Imru' al-Qays); and (b) the purely descriptive ... The milieu is aristocratic and the full panoply of hunting animals and techniques is celebrated. (*EAL*)

The Saluki, the cheetah, the goshawk, the tiercel gos, the saker, the peregrine, and the merlin: these are the animals to which individual poems are devoted. The animals that were hunted are described in relatively less detail; these include the hare, the fox, the gazelle, the crane and the bustard. (In the artistic subordination of hunted fauna to the animals of the chase these poems contrast with the detailed engraved artwork on modern hunting rifles which tend to depict the game [in its glory before its destruction]: geese, ducks, pheasants, deer, boars, lions and elephants, etc. It is a notable inversion.)

A Saluki Hound

> "the *saluki*, pendulous-eared, hound, who hunted entirely by sight – only rarely mentioned by name, ... though this was without doubt the only canine to have been used in the chase" (Lyons)

There are nine authentic, and a further twenty-eight possibly speciously ascribed, *urjuzas* about hounds alone in Abu Nuwas's *Diwan*. With the extraordinary energy it conveys of the animal raring to go, pulling at the leash, "champing at the bit" at the crack of dawn, the following is a fine representative example of the vigor and ethos of the *tardiyya*. The poem exists in two versions. Both are given below to show how texts can be scrambled with time. Several lines are identical; others, the later ones especially, are quite distinct, taking the poems in the end in different directions. The second version may be a variant or even corruption of the first (though it has its very own qualities); or it may be a copy by another author inspired by the original. One simply cannot be certain. While the first has the prestige of being, apparently, the more authentic poem, they are cast from similar molds and stimulated by the same passion. And both give an excellent idea of the great stamina of the Saluki, which had already been used in pre-Islamic and Umayyad times.

Poem I: (there is some confusion about the first two lines of the poem – below is one possible reading):

> When morning appeared from behind its veil
>> Like the figure of a greying man from his robe (*Jilbab*)
> …
> And like an Abyssinian grinning to reveal his teeth,
>> We stirred with a dog we have long met the day with
> He almost left the leash in tatters with his lurching,
>> Heaving with uncontrolled excitement
>> – with the energy that commanded his youth;
> When he strutted forwards the two lines along his back
>> Were like a pair of snakes slinking briskly forwards;
> His claws, sheathed inside their paws,
>> Were like the razors of a cupper ensconced in their scabbard;
> When the hunter called out to him as he ran
>> He almost sprang from his own hide;
> The valley floor resounded with his pace
>> At which he seemed to be leaving the ground.
> He was like a drunkard (one we relied upon [for provisions])
>> Effacing his traces by dragging his clothes along the soil*
> All but those marks traced by the very fringes of his garment.

---

* The medieval editor glosses this line in more detail even than other lines: "He wipes out the traces, i.e., he is saying that this dog pares the earth while running, his belly wiping out the traces of his fore- and hind legs, thus his paw prints end up looking like the tracks of a drunkard who has dragged his clothes along the ground effacing them…"

Pasturing animals were rounded up by him,
Like prisoners of war to his claws and his fangs. (*D*. ii, 187–9)

Poem II:

When morning appeared from behind its veil
    And night returned whence it came
The hunter harnessed him and set off,
    Restraining him when he pulled at the leash –
At times constraining the intractable beast
    Then relaxing his hold whenever he gave.
He bared his fangs to reveal
    Whetted blades and spearheads;
The eyes which he glared from
    Were like carnelian gems convening upon his face;
His upper chest heaved from his breast-girth
    Draping down as he held his nose to the ground.
After reaching the summit of a slope, or half-way,
    And casting a glance quickly around
At the wonders of gardens in the valley basin
    Where herds of animals had appeared,
He dispatched him like an arrow; he was more than this:
    Zealous and faster than the blinking of an eye,
Sprinting down to the valley floor
    At a pace that almost flayed his own hide.
He flashed like lightning in the clouds
    Until he was almost … no more
And the hunter called out to him from his now distant spot
    Scolding this uncontrolled attack*
When the prey had been thrown into the dust he chided him
        again
    And the dog turned back towards the voice that had called
        him.

These were restless hounds, fervent for the chase, as captured brilliantly in the following image: "I shall describe a
hound pulling on his tether, like a madman fleeing from having
medicine introduced up his nose …" (trans. Rex Smith).

* ? – The text is uncertain here

The Cheetah

There is just one fully authentic *urjuza* about the cheetah in the *Diwan* (in the critical edition five further poems on the cheetah are given in a section of poems deemed less reliable by the redactor, al-Isfahani).* We can recognize the first line as formulaic; but the continuation is as relatively rare as the animal it describes.

(*Textual Note.* The essayist al-Jahiz [d. 869] ascribes a substantially similar poem to one al-Raqashi [d. c. 815] in his "Book of Animals". This is suspect, *and* ironical, since the two poets couldn't stand each other; but it is also understandable since they shared much in the way of poetic temperament. The ascription to Abu Nuwas has greater authority, but since al-Jahiz is such an early source it is hard to discredit him altogether. The issue of authenticity often has one turning in circles; and so it is wise at times to draw a sponge across the matter, insouciantly – to read the poetry that is otherwise trapped in a philologist's limbo.)

> I would set off at dawn,(– when the night was [still dark]
>> Like a cloud blocking sight
>>> Yet morning made headway upon the shadows,
>> Slicing through the dimness like a sword finely wrought –)
>>> With a beast, broad jawed, swift and energetic,
>> Stout in frame, with a strapping back and heavy set
>>> Yet taut, lean, and tapering in at the waist
>> Vicious to look at! Ample folds on bright cheeks
>>> Black at the base of the ears and the root of the jaws
>> Broad-muzzled like a Bactrian camel over a rosy collar
>>> With large paws and razor-sharp claws
>> Like a lion yet with stippled coat
>>> Ready to pounce on any moving figure

* * *

---

* There are earlier and later examples in Abu al-Najm al-'Ijli and Ibn al-Mu'tazz, respectively.

After an extensive look around he spotted
  Two herds of gazelle appearing on a hard flatland
  So he set off to stalk them at a furtive pace;
He crept along, sneaking up unawares,
  Gliding forward like a male viper
Over raised and hollow terrain,
  Then when poised before the quarry
He scattered them upon the even ground
  Wreaking carnage with lacerating tears.

* * *

After a period of want and economy
  There is no benefit from a hunt without a cheetah.
    (D. ii, 200–202)

In fascinating and pertinent remarks one scholar writes:

In his "Book of Taming the Wild Beasts of the Desert" the writer
Muhammad ibn al-Mankli (d. 1384) describes the process of
capturing and training a cheetah in great detail. A professional
cheetah-keeper (*fahhad*) and his assistants had to track down,
subdue, and train adult animals since they did not give birth in
captivity. The trickiest part of this process was teaching the
cheetah, a creature so indolent that an Arabic proverb, "sleepier
than a cheetah", was coined after it, to ride a horse to the hunt
(at the front of the keeper's saddle).
…
Al-Mankli also described the cheetahs of Iraq, among
them those … of Samawah, who are: "very beautiful, mostly
white, with small spots, light bodied and long-boned" and
whose "backs and tails are long. When they appear their necks
look like dice and when they retreat their backs are like snakes,
and their tails, when they hold them up, are like spears."
(*World Literature and Its Times*, vol. 6, art. "Abu Nuwas",
Mark Wagner)

By the time al-Mankli was writing, some of his vivid impres-
sions had the ring of five centuries.

Elegy for a Hound

While out hunting, Abu Nuwas's hound, Hallab, was bitten by a snake and died. He wrote this elegy on the occasion. As with all elegies, the language is accessible and less intricately descriptive than the average hunting poem. It is also more particular, depicting a specific occasion in the second half, and denuded of some of the formulaic language associated with the poems that lie closer to the median-line of the "genre".

> Poor dog! – He was a lord among hounds!
> He fulfilled my need of a falcon,
> Took the place of butcher
> And stockpiling quartermaster.
> Among the throngs of ruddy white gazelles, dogs
> And every rampant catcher,
> He snatched hill-dwelling fauna
> Quick as a lightning flash glimpsed mid star and cloud.
> How many a lean-flanked gazelle
> Who came and went defiantly
> Did he provide me with for grilled meat?
> I set out with him when the world rested,
> My teeth and utensils still
> Yellow-stained from the saffron cooking of a previous catch,
> As if greased lightly with liquid gold.
> There we were, in the thicket,
> When, lo, a serpent appeared baring its fangs,
> Striped and naked of all covering,
> And staring through its facial mask.
> It dug its fangs into my poor hound's hocks
> And showed no partiality for me –
> O would I had not returned without punishment
> … Not before you had tasted the most painful chastisement!
> (D. ii, 280)

An elegant introduction to this genre, showcasing Abu Nuwas in particular, is Rex Smith's "Hunting Poetry (*Tardiyyat*)". The poetic devices employed are described succinctly (simile, metaphor, metonymy [here reference to animals according to adjectival qualities rather than generic nouns], and hyperbole), followed by extensive translated excerpts with valuable explanatory notes. We learn, for example, about the consistent zoological accuracy of Abu Nuwas's observations; e.g., the saker, in one poem, is

> ... *spotted between the back and the throat, her primaries little distinguished one from another at the extremities, nimble.*
> ... The primaries are the feathers at the end of the wings, the main flying feathers; on the saker they are found close together, though in some birds of prey they can be spaced out with clear gaps between them.
> Abu Nuwas ... must have gained wide practical experience on the hunting field, for technical faults are negligible and the work utterly convincing.

The Polo Match

Abu Nuwas did not confuse hunting with polo. After giving in full twenty-six "genuine" hunting *urjuzas* and four "genuine" hunting *qasidas*, al-Isfahani relays five anomalous poems about whose authorship he was uncertain. These poems were apparently lumped together precisely because of their unusual contents which did not fit snugly within any of the main generic categories of the *Diwan*. Since the first and second poems are allusive and veiled descriptions of a penis and a dirham, respectively, borrowing the imagery of a *saker* falcon, al-Isfahani placed them here – *faute de mieux*. It is the subject matter which appears to have cast doubt in his mind as to the authenticity of the five poems. But the editorial reflex is not entirely convincing and the poem about polo is one of the exquisite curios of the *Diwan*. It is imbued with the amateurism (in the real sense) and energy of a hunt, and is a quite fabulous piece of descriptive verse.

(In English the first three lines, delineating the pedigree of the players, read like clutter; in Arabic such expression has elegance and succinctness – it is itself, in a sense, part of the pedigree of the society depicted.)

Noble Men

And I might watch the pleasures of bright young men,
　From among the descendants of al-'Abbas, lords of men,
Or the tribes of Qahtan or Mudar;
　Or simply an intimate friend who gives shelter
A face enhanced by good repute.

Riders, Sticks and Balls

　They were all mounted on steeds as exquisite as a picture
Lean noble stallions, issue of A'waj,
　Not cauterized by the farrier to treat overfeeding.
The players were like Jinn upon Jinn, even if they were only
　　men,
　As if stitched to their mounts with needle [and thread]
Or it was as if the rider was riveted to his pony
　In a verdant field as lush as striped garments
Laurelled with splendor and pride
　And so on a cold and chilly day,
When the sun shone after a downpour of rain
　They took out polo sticks at which the eye marveled
Their extremities perfectly curved and bent round
　Faultlessly measured by craftsmen
Neither too long nor too short.
　The players called out, hitting the balls to each other
Smooth balls with plaited seams
　Bound tightly around a stuffing of hair
That had been expertly made by the artisan
　Wielding a bone awl deftly, stitching,
Leaving not a trace of the tool upon the surface of the ball
　One would think it was an apple dangling from the tree!

The Climax of the Game

When the [players on one team] had closed off the danger
　They delegated the bravest among them for the fight
One tested in battle, fugitive from a near death,
　Distinguished by his skill, famous for clean strokes
Fair-minded, with a restless eye,
　A leader of significance to captain the team;
He drove the ball on, then struck it forwards [and high]

And it fell like a star dropping from the sky,
Up and down, the ball bobbed at a steady rhythm
  Hit onwards with keen and solid strokes
Like arrows propelled by the string of a bow.
  Among these normally self-possessed and dignified men,
You could see many now snorting like beasts when the ball was
      struck sweetly
  And the man dying for victory shouted out and screamed.
And the soul of the man who fears the vicissitudes of Time
      despaired
  They knew they where beaten or trounced.
…

The Lesson (for Player and Pundit)

In order for those who place bets to win
  Some are hard done by and others delight;
Such are the vagaries of Time and Fate! (*D.* ii, 256–7)

The circumstances of the game are given briefly in the *Diwan*. In the town of Isabadh, Abu Nuwas was in the company of al-'Abbas ibn Musa al-Hadi when they came across Zuhayr ibn Musayyab and Saqr ibn Malik, of the tribe of Khuza'a, stick-and-balling on the main square. He joined the players who divided up into two teams. In the end, the poet won these noblemen over and joined them for food and drink after the game, composing this poem about the contest in a merry state.

It is a rare, perhaps unique, poem. Yet it conforms in several ways to the tradition of poetry, particularly in the epigrammatic ending about time and fate — a lesson to be drawn even from a game of polo. Like all the best poetry, there is a mixture of formula and utter invention: the nobility of the players, as already intimated, is somewhat well-worn but the description of, for example, how these expert horsemen stayed on the saddle (like genies sown or riveted to their mounts), and the quality of the polo-balls, seamlessly sown, are the descriptive jewels of this piece. Two further things might be noted.

1. First, the fine linguistic quality of Qur'anic evocation to describe the champion hitter:

> He drove the ball on, then struck it forwards [and high]
>> And it fell like a star dropping from the sky.

The Arabic for "drove" here is *daha*; it is a Qur'anic verb used for God's "spreading out" of the land in Sura 79 referring to creation. The allusion is unmistakable, especially in combination with the image of the "dropping star", which employs apocalyptic language borrowed most notably from Sura 81. One can view this either simply as part of the enhanced linguistic texture of the poem, underscoring with lofty scriptural association the lauded qualities of the player; or introducing the serious cadence of the poem's ending. Or both, conceivably. We should be reminded, in any case, that Abu Nuwas's poetry generally is studded with Qur'anic evocations of just this quality.

The euphony of this and the following line in Arabic is superb, evoking with repeated word patterns and sounds the smooth, energetic and constant movement of the ball; one can sense this even without knowledge of the language:

> *Bikuratin daha biha thumma zajar*
>> *Fa-nhadarat ka-l-najmi walla fa-nkadarat*
> *Raf'an wa-wad'an ayyuma dhaka staqar*
>> *Tudfa'u bi-l-darbi idha l-darbu stamar.*

2. In the ethos of this culture, forbearance and self-control were cardinal virtues, as they had been in pre-Islamic Arabia (and the Near East in general). How expressive of the excitement of a game, therefore, that even a man of forbearance should scream and shout with abandon, desperate for a win when the game is – apparently – played down to the wire. The poem is structured, one might say, to convey the nail-biting ordeal.

5

"POETRY FOR MORTALS AND THE DEAD"

On the Ascetic Poem and the Elegy

THE ASCETIC POEM

Scholars imbued with medieval Arab notions of poetic tax-
onomy might balk at placing the ascetic poem (*zuhdiyya*) and
the elegy (*marthiya*) side by side, for medieval commentators
considered the elegy to be a form of panegyric (*madih*): it was
praise of the dead, with the accent being on "praise" rather than
"the dead". But the fact is: the elegy and ascetic poem have
death in common, and the subject is not easily ignored. There are
twenty-four ascetic poems in the critical edition of the *Diwan*.
At least five other poems can be added to his extant output if
one includes poems of less reliable attribution. One of the very
finest of all these, and one, ironically, whose authorship is
uncertain, is a funeral song for the poet's own self. Abu Nuwas,
or his silver-penned ghost-writer, imagines himself vividly
after his own death; the tone is very much elegiac, with more
than a hint of self-pity.

> Bear patiently up to the vagaries of Fate
>> Perchance you will be grateful for the outcome …
> Prepare your self/soul before its decease,
>> Begin saving for the Day when
>> Our "savings" are tallied against us

* * *

It will seem as if your family calls out to you
  (But you will not hear, exhaling your death rattle);
As if they have anointed you
  With perfumes which the dead take for store;
And as if they have turned you over upon your bed
  Then over into the darkness of the grave.

* * *

O would that I knew how you will fare
  Unwitting upon your bed;
Or that I knew how you will fare
  When [your body] is bathed in camphor and lotus blossom;
Or that I knew how you will fare
  When account is made on the Morning of Assembly

* * *

What will be my defense about the things I have done?
  What will I say to my Lord? What excuse will mine be –
For not having sought out a path of righteousness,
  Or embracing the [good] I turned my back on?
O for the misery of my returns –
  And the pity of what was missed of my life!
      (D. ed. Ghazali, 609–10)

There is a simple structural enchantment about these
verses. It has a preamble, followed by two paired segments of
three lines each, and a conclusion – a perfect symmetrical
arrangement. The central diptych of three-line sections features anaphora, that is, each verse begins with an identical formula. This rhetorical kind of repetition is a characteristic of
ascetic poetry and can generate the effect of litany.

Imagining his own death had been a heroic posture of the
early Arab poet, before Islam. For the pre-Islamic poet, furthermore, the situation was similar when, in some of the most
moving short scenes of the early canon, he identified with the
hungry desert wolf, alone, emaciated, and on the point of death
on bitter cold nights. But imagining death and then conjuring
up a time far beyond that point is Islamic. The two kinds of
poetry have a radically different feel.

"Savings" (scilicet, stored up for recompense in the Afterlife) are a standard metaphor for pious acts. The Judgment is in this sense the archetype of a rainy day. "Savings" (Ar. *dhakhr*) are interchangeable or synonymous with "provisions" (Ar. *zad*). Death, the grave, Judgment, pious "savings": these, among other elements, are all basic constituents of the *zuhdiyya* (– which is not, it should be stressed, religious in the sense of *theological*; there is as much theology in the decadent wine poem, if not more.) The poem, however, is exceptionally eloquent, grouping a few standard ideas around two emotively charged scenes (death and Judgment), sketched vividly yet with linguistic and descriptive economy.

The *zuhdiyya* is a minor genre, though it basks vicariously in the prestige of religion. With roots in a certain kind of universal wisdom to be found already in pre-Islamic poetry, notably the verse of the Christian poet 'Adi ibn Zayd (d. *c.* 600), and with precursors among a small handful of early Islamic poets, it was developed into a fully fledged independent genre by Abu al-'Atahiya (d. 826), who was by turns a literary companion and antagonist of Abu Nuwas. With its uncomplicated pietistic message centered on the ephemeral nature of material existence, it is the hardest genre in which to be original. It is perhaps no accident that it is associated principally with just one poet. The extraordinary fact about Abu al-'Atahiya is that he was able, with easy fluency, to compose over 5,000 verses from a *relatively* restricted repertory of ideas. While he was unquestionably a gifted poet (and uniquely prodigious in a single genre), he also sensed that his preferred register was not beyond the talents and inspiration of Abu Nuwas. Below are selected some of the more inventive ideas from the latter's few ascetic poems.

A Righteous Dowry

... The young man refuses all but to follow capricious passion
Though the path of Truth is clear to him.

> Raise up your eyes towards women
>> Whose dowries will be your righteous acts;
> Only a man whose balance weighs heavily
>> Will lead the houri out from her veiled enclosure. (D. ii, 158)

The metaphor of the scales of judgment is Qur'anic. In the short apocalyptic Sura 101, for example, the scales that measure deeds on Judgment Day are weighted heavily with the virtuous acts of people and lightly with the bad.

The poem produces an apposite image to reform the philandering male, conjuring marriage in the afterlife to the houris of Paradise in return for the dowry of an upright earthly life, principally a life of chastity. Abu Nuwas was speaking the language of a debauched man, whether as himself or someone else.

Man's Mortal Genealogy

In Abbasid society Arab tribal genealogy (nasab) retained some of the importance it had had in earlier periods. The Arab tribes who had arrived as conquerors in the Near East outside Arabia in the seventh century continued to provide a language of social membership and prestige. A small number of families descending, or claiming to descend, from these tribes were still around in the flesh, as prestigious as people who sailed to America on the Mayflower. But more importantly, a vast number of people, mostly of non-Arab origin, remembered or claimed to remember having an ancestor or patron who was an Arab tribesman and who thus gave them a tribe to identify with. Abu Nuwas fell into this category. It does not mean that these tribes existed in any real sense of the word. They did not have chiefs, tribal lands, or collective interests; they did not engage in collective action; they were not real political or social groups – just memories and after-images. It was in this context that people were commonly versed in knowledge of the forefathers of the "tribes", often going back to their eponymous ancestors. The ascetic poem sought to deflate the importance of these

allegiances, cutting this sense of *nasab* down to size and pro-
moting an "all-men-are-equal" type ethos:

> I see that every living person is Mortal, son of Mortal
> With a prestigious lineage among the dead (*D.* ii, 159)

This is cited from a poem that contains one of Abu Nuwas's
most admired ascetic lines:

> If the clever man examines the world,
> He will discover a foe dressed up as a friend

His poetry could elicit keen appreciation, not least from the
paragon of the genre himself, Abu al-'Atahiya, who is recorded
as saying: "Sixteen thousand verses have entered into the public
domain from among my ascetic poems but I wish that Abu
Nuwas would attribute just one of his verses to me, along with
two others, in return for a thousand verses of my own ..."
The two poets were mutual admirers – when, that is, Abu
al-'Atahiya wasn't deluded by paranoia into thinking that
Abu Nuwas was encroaching on his poetic turf.

The Danger of Empty Talk

The *zuhdiyya* promotes an etiquette of ascetic comportment,
though in a somewhat rudimentary fashion; that is to say,
cumulatively as a collection of materials and not according to a
methodical manifesto. In this general scheme idle talk is viewed
as a symptom of the perishable material world:

> ... Better a death from the sickness of silence
> Than from the sickness of chatter;
> How often you have loosened up with banter
> The bolts that lock away death ... (*D.* ii, 164)

Eloquent Simplicity

The *zuhdiyya* is the most linguistically accessible of the genres
of classical Arabic poetry; the medieval philologists and editors

had far less need to gloss the language with explanations of meaning – of the kind they provided for other genres, especially the densely descriptive ones like the hunting poem which tended to use a difficult archaizing lexicon. Abu al-'Atahiya's poetry is reputed to have been popular in his day among the people of the market place precisely because he wrote in an appealing language that was quite within their grasp. It was a relatively simple register of formal poetry whose own particular eloquence was a consequence of its plain-spoken style. A phrase in medieval Arabic literary criticism, going back at least to the tenth century, was coined to describe writing that is at once easy to read and understand and yet hard to emulate: *al-sahl al-mumtani'* ("the inimitably easy"). Abu Hilal al-'Askari (d. 1005) uses it in a well-known saying, though the concept is considerably older. It describes the *zuhdiyya* to a tee.

The poem translated in full below is an elegant ascetic meditation. It is a reiteration of the uncomplicated, collective wisdom of the pious and devout; the acoustics of the Arabic are soft and musical, accentuated by internal rhyme and assonance in the first three lines; the syntax is succinct, the lexicon and semantics straightforward. It is structured in three parts: an opening triplet, a central verse of devotion, and a closing triplet. The first and third parts have internal, and respectively distinct, phonetic, morphological and semantic cohesion. Thus the poem has what one might call perfect balance. To the cynical and discontent it might read as simplistic, to the pious and sensitive, more convincingly, it is unassuming and has the appeal of simple eloquence.

> Every mourner will be mourned
>> Every weeper will be wept for
> Every saving will be spent
>> And every memory forgotten
> Only God remains
>> Whosoever is exalted, God is more exalted

* * *

He has provided our sustenance – O Lord!
    We suffer and strive for Him

* * *

Good and evil have features
    That cannot be concealed
Whosoever hides behind a cover
    In God's sight will be revealed
None of the things you see
    Can be hidden from God (*D*. ii, 169–70)

Sound and Meaning

We have encountered this fact already: the *zuhdiyya* apostrophizes man and encourages him to reflect. This effect is achieved in a uniquely engaging way in the opening two verses of a poem; they are truncated, ending elliptically, in such a fashion that the reader is forced to complete both the meaning and the syntax:

Be with God and He will be there for you
    And be God-fearing, so that you may …
You should be nothing other
    Than prepared for the Fates, as if … (*D*. ii, 170)

According to the commentary contained in one of the manuscripts of the *Diwan*, the lines imply: "fear God *so that you may survive*, prepare for death *as if you are already dead*."

In stark contrast with their unfinished syntax, the first two lines are acoustically overdetermined. The rhyme letter, the guttural "k" (Ar. *Kaf* – the dominant consonant of the entire poem), is the Arabic second person singular pronominal suffix "*–ka*" (in poetry, for prosodic reasons, the suffix may lose its vowel: "*–k*", as here, resembling thus spoken Arabic). The strong acoustics of the guttural phoneme, which is stressed by internal repetition within the line, amplifies the semantics of apostrophe, addressing the poem's imaginary audience and

obliging a response to the enigma of the missing verse endings.
One can sense the aural effect even in transcription:

> Kun ma'a llahi yaKun laK
> > Wa-ttaQi llaha la'allaK ...
> La taKun illa mu'iddan
> > li-l-manaya fa-Ka'annaK ...

The poem thus has both overt and subliminal rhetoric each
of which is dependent on the other.

The Permanent Ink of the Angels

The most ambivalent of ascetic poems and one which al-Suli
was inclined to categorize among the poems of *mujun* (ribaldry) is the following:

> There is a sin which a man will desire full value from
> > And hearty praise, and to be placed frankly in its lineage
> He does not grind his teeth with regret for it,
> > He stands proudly upright among the people;
> Whenever he remembers it, his imagination gets the better
> > of him
> Such that anger may affect him due to his great pride.
> The angels have recorded it with their hands
> > Against me, and The Days do not efface what they have
> > > written. (*D.* ii, 172–3)

According to Islamic belief, angels record the sins of men on
scrolls (Qur'anic *suhuf*) that are unfolded and read on
Judgment Day. "The Days" (Ar. *al-Ayyam*) are a standard agent
in Arabic poetry of Time's erosion. It is no clearer in the original Arabic of this poem what sin Abu Nuwas is referring to
than it is in the English. That is left to *our* surmise. But there is a
tension built into this poem: it would seem that the final line is
intended to destabilize and threaten the insouciance and reckless pride of the first three. A note of volatility – of the
ephemeral – is struck in the third line: the poet's pride is now
mixed with anger. Thus, faced with the steady and immutable

written record of his sin, will he not come to rue his debauched conceit? Or is he rather challenging the immutable world with his pride? This kind of ambivalence is one of the defining features of Abu Nuwas's poetry.

* * * * *

THE ELEGY

In pre-Islamic Arabia women of the tribe sang funerary laments in rhymed prose bewailing the dead. Poetry may have developed from this practice, in particular as a medium to encourage the taking of vengeance for those murdered or killed in battle. The dynamic which evolved for this poetry, one of the earliest independent genres, was made up of two elements: the invocation and license to "break the social constraint" of patience and forbearance (in order to cry and show grief), and praise for the deceased. In the Umayyad period the elegy came to be composed for "distinguished public personalities"; thus in addition to having the personal, effusive aspect of its earlier form it became a "tool of political or religious rhetoric" (*EAL*, art. "Marthiya", G. Borg). Abu Nuwas wrote laments for both friends and political figures. But since the latter tended also to be friends or close associates, for instance the caliph al-Amin, there is a fair measure of spontaneity in most of the surviving poems which may explain in part their near fractured, or relatively unstructured, nature. Abu Nuwas's elegies are distinct from the greatest or most classic examples of the genre – the numerous dirges of the poetess al-Khansa' (d. 665) for her brother, Sakhr, or the neoclassical elegance of al-Mutanabbi's elegy for his grandmother with its admixture of genuine sorrow, utter self-absorption and accomplished linguistic rhetoric. It is fair to say that Abu Nuwas is seldom cited as a leading figure of the genre; his poems in this category are just as interesting as biographical, and even historical, documentary shards.

For Harun al-Rashid (d. 809)

People are divided between the glad and the saddened
    And the sick man who is ransom to the palm of death;
But who now can be gladdened with this world and its gaiety
    After [the passing of] the blessed Harun? (*D.* i, 299)

(Abu Nuwas also wrote consoling "Abu al-'Abbas" al-Fadl ibn
Rabi' upon the death of al-Rashid, but the lines read not so
much as elegy for al-Rashid as encouragement to show alle-
giance to his son and successor, al-Amin.)

For Muhammad ibn Zubayda "al-Amin" (d. 813)

Death has folded away what was between Muhammad and me;
    No one can unfurl that which death has folded.
There is no union now, just tears prolonged
    By [memories I] cannot hold back;
I used to be wary of death for him alone;
    There is nothing left now about which to care;
While houses are inhabited by those I dislike
    The graveyard is inhabited by my loved one. (*D.* i, 299)

Two other fragments survive for al-Amin. One contains the
line: "*Was it not possible for people who have not died to die // And for
death's appointment to be driven from you to me?*" – which is poignant
(and prescient) as Abu Nuwas died not long afterwards.

For the Barmecides

Passing by the palaces of the Rabi' family, who had been the
Barmecides greatest political rivals, Abu Nuwas lamented:

... Fate did not watch over the rights of Yahya al-Barmaki
    Except as one watching over the dues of Rabi'. (*D.* i, 300)

And passing by the former palaces of the Barmecides the
poet wrote upon a random wall:

These are the Barmecides who learnt
    The behavior of kings and taught it to the people.

When they sowed they [also] watered and when they built
   No foundation ever crumbled,
And when they ever did something for men
   They clothed it in a mantle of permanence. (D. i, 301)

Fragment for His Son

On the morning of its return Death left no one for us
   In whom we could rejoice
It is as if I offended death with [the] son I was blessed with
   When I had grown old and grey (D. i, 301)

Adding to the poignancy of this shard about a child effaced
from the world is that we know scarcely more about Abu
Nuwas's son than what these verses tersely communicate.

For Waliba ibn al-Hubab

When Abu Nuwas's tutor died he (Waliba) would have had no
cause to regret missing out on life's pleasures. It is interesting
to see therefore what tone the poem takes; it is written in the
so-called "Complete" meter (Kamil), but a shortened form of
it, more suitable for light verses. The language is simple and
unaffected; the rhyme pattern in Arabic established by the dead
man's name, Waliba.

(Translator's Caveat. This translation suffers from the fact that,
short though they are, each line is a syntactic unit; this exacer-
bates in English a sense of abruptness in the thematic transitions
from line to line, and is not an uncommon problem in the less
felicitous translations of early Arabic poetry.)

Your tears have poured copiously
   With grief at the death of Waliba;
At Abu Usama's death the wailing woman
   Stood up among his companions
To publicize his noble acts
   Without lie or fabrication;
Banu Asad has been afflicted,

Banu Nizar wears a frown [of distress];
[They have] lost their spokesman and leader
    In times of calamity or stress;
Do not go far, Abu Usama,
    For death is a necessity;
Every man is assaulted
    By its striking arrows;
Annihilation was prescribed for [God's] servants:
    Every soul is leaving;
How many a brother you have left behind
    With lasting anguish over you;
Before your death each one thought it
    Too immense [a matter] that you be struck down by
        disaster. (*D.* i, 309)

Just as moving as this elegy was Abu Nuwas's terse reaction on hearing of Waliba's death: "Today good-mannered wit and erudition have died." This, one may infer, is how one should understand the decadent life of a poet such as Waliba: that within the bravado of excess (in word and perhaps even deed) was the elegant and indelible heart of wit and learning.

For A Sick Friend

Willy nilly
    My heart is sickened by your illness;
May the Merciful turn harm aside from you
    And may the evil Fates appear for me instead ...

... After He Died

Two intimate friends were created for union
    And their union coalesced in love;
They were like two branches off a trunk
    But were divided by the vagaries of Time,
Their stalks turned yellow having been green
    Which caused the leaves to fall off their branches. (*D.* i, 308)

The expression here may strike one as abstract and impersonal. But the language is uncomplicated, which can be a sign of sincerity; and the short poem has its own acoustic quality: the sustained assonance of long "a" in Arabic which complements the grammatical (and semantic) use of the dual form. The sound of the poem puts stress on two when one of two has gone.

Again for Himself

This chapter began with such a piece — a perhaps spuriously attributed poem which one editor has described as being of such beauty that it was just as likely to be by Abu Nuwas as any other poet. My feeling is that in this case the authorship may be beside the point: it is a superb and eloquent example of Abbasid self-effacement. As we come full circle in "Poetry for Mortals and the Dead" with self-elegy, the argument needs hardly to be made further that the *zuhdiyya* and the *marthiya* share an essential register.

There are in fact a number of elegant and ornamentally bare laments of self written apparently when Abu Nuwas lay sickly and dying:

> Annihilation has crept into m[y] lower and upper [parts],
>   I see that I am dying limb after limb
> No hour passes me by except that
>   It reduces me by a fraction in passing;
> Along with my strength self obeisance has abandoned me
>   As I remember now, weakened and emaciated, obeisance
>   to God
> How I regret those nights and days
>   Full spent in amusement and play;
> We committed every wicked deed;
>   May God forgive, pardon and give us reprieve. (D. i, 302)

He sent the following poem to a friend while suffering from the illness that would kill him:

> The poetry of a dead man has come to you in the words of
>   one living

Who has come to stand [at the junction] between life and
death;
Fate's "Events" have wasted his body such that
He is now almost invisible to the eyes of these "Events" –
If you look at me to perceive my features
You will not grasp a single word of the book of my face …
(D. i, 302)

* * * * *

When Abu Nuwas was living that pleasure-seeking life for
which he is famous and which he wrote up in his euphoric and
often decadent lyric poems, he saw the glass of life half full. The
focus simply shifted when, prompted by a religious sensibility
or the demands of being a complete poet, the glass of life was
seen as half empty, the pleasures of life delusional, and the
poetry became the reminder to the living that they are mortal.
The religious aspect of this issued from the same basic fact. It
seems morose but it is true, as it is undoubtedly also true that
the particular aesthetic beauty of the poetry can even make one
forget the pall of this often doleful register.

There are various brief accounts of his epitaph. It is
reported, for instance, that upon his shroud was embroidered
the confession: "My excuse, Lord, will be to admit that I have
no excuse." This is personal, yet much of his ascetic poetry
could be adopted as a universal epitaph for humankind

… Man disappears from view
Until it seems as if his movements
Were formed originally from the very stillness (D. ii, 172)

"WALK THE EVEN
PATH WITH ME ..."
AN AFTERWORD

Among the works of medieval Arabic literature analogous with
Dante's *Divine Comedy*, which encapsulated for posterity the literary influence of certain individuals, is the *Epistle of Familiar
Spirits (Risalat al-Tawabi' wa-l-Zawabi')* by the Cordoban poet
Ibn Shuhayd (d. 1035). The interest of this work in general "lies
in its imaginative premise. Following the tradition of the *mi'raj*
[the Prophet Muhammad's visit to heaven and hell], the poet
travels with his inspiring genius to the netherworld to meet the
jinn of poets living and deceased, engaging – and besting –
them in poetic competition. The narration becomes a literary
commentary on the Parnassus of Arabic poets ..." (*EAL*, art.
"Ibn Shuhayd"). Among the encounters with the muses of seven
poets, representing both the Ancients and the Moderns, there
is one with "Husayn", the demon muse of Abu Nuwas. The
scene is set up briefly as follows. Ibn Shuhayd travels in the
company of his own poetic muse, Zuhayr. They come across a
large monastery, surrounded by outlying churches and taverns,
and recognize it as Dayr Hanna, the monastery of a place
known as Dhat al-Ukayrah; both names feature in the poetry of
Abu Nuwas. They inquire after "Husayn" and are warned by
monks that he is inebriated in a tavern; but the visitors insist on
meeting him. Zuhayr now advises Ibn Shuhayd to recite one of
his tavern poems in order to stir the drunken demon from his
stupor. Five lines of bacchic poetry are at this point inserted
into the narrative; the lines are competent within the norms of
the genre and generally reminiscent of Abu Nuwas, though
they are not particularly memorable. "Husayn" recognizes the
verses, vaguely, as those of Ibn Shuhayd and subsequently an
exchange of poetry, touching on a number of subjects, ensues
between the two figures.

Husayn goes on to recite some of the poetry with which he has inspired Abu Nuwas (from the latter's *Diwan*); he then asks Ibn Shuhayd to recite more verses of his own, but the latter replies, "Have you left anything subject to be versified?" (which was something of a recurring anxiety among poets). The demon's reply is significant. "You *must* recite! But walk the even path with me and avoid the highlands." The reference is ultimately to the terrains of Arabia: to rugged uplands and level plains, a metaphor for poetic expression that was either harsh and rugged or smooth, refined, even urbane. "Husayn" is asking for poetry like "his" own, and the statement is in fact Ibn Shuhayd's understated but important recognition of Abu Nuwas's extraordinary stylistic influence on the Arabic tradition. It is *style* as much as *theme* that is important in this respect, as evinced by the compositions of two of the most well-known Andalusian poets of the eleventh century, Ibn Zaydun and al-Mu'tamid ibn 'Abbad; in different ways they, and others, were deeply indebted to Abu Nuwas's often mellifluous verse. A few decades later the stanzaic lyric poems (*muwashshaha*s) of al-A'ma al-Tutili (the Blind Toledan, d. 1130) are so redolent of Abu Nuwas that they read like conscious tributes – which is significant since Abu Nuwas's habit of quoting other poets (and even himself) in the last line of his lyric poems may have influenced a similar, and historically very significant feature at the structural tail-end of the Andalusian *muwashshaha*.

The point of illustrating Abu Nuwas's literary afterlife through Ibn Shuhayd is that whilst he is – typically – associated, according to a sort of standard reflex, with the theme of the tavern, the *style* is more subtly just as important as the tavern: Abu Nuwas, coarse and eccentric though he could be, steered a stylistically natural and "even path" at the very heart of the classical Arabic tradition of poetry.

Contemporary Arab authors are profoundly sensitive to Abu Nuwas, none more so than the eminent Sudanese novelist, Tayeb Salih. There are evocations of Abu Nuwas in several of his works, including the celebrated *Season of Migration to the North*.

In the following excerpt the protagonist of the novel, Mustafa Sa'eed, who is the troubled incarnation of a conflict between cultures (British and Sudanese, colonizer and colonized), describes how he came across one of his English girlfriends:

> I had met her following a lecture I gave in Oxford on Abu Nuwas. I told them that Omar Khayyam was nothing in comparison with Abu Nuwas. I read them some of his poetry about wine in comic oratorical style which I claimed was how Arabic poetry used to be recited in the Abbasid era. In the lecture I said that Abu Nuwas was a Sufi mystic and that he had made of wine a symbol with which to express all his spiritual yearnings, that the longing for wine in his poetry was really a longing for self-obliteration in the Divine – all arrant nonsense with no basis in fact. However, I was inspired that evening and found the lies tripping off my tongue like sublime truths. Feeling that my elation was communicating itself to my audience, I lied more and more extravagantly. After the lecture they all crowded round me: retired civil servants who had worked in the East, old women whose husbands had died in Egypt, Iraq and the Sudan, men who had fought with Kitchener and Allenby, orientalists, and officials in the Colonial Office and the Middle Eastern section of the Foreign Office. Suddenly I saw a girl of eighteen or nineteen rushing towards me through the ranks of people. She put her arms round me and kissed me. "You are beautiful beyond description," she said, speaking in Arabic, "and the love I have for you is beyond description." With an emotion the violence of which frightened me, I said: "At last I have found you, Sausan. I searched everywhere for you and was afraid I would never find you. Do you remember?" "How can I forget our house in Karkh in Baghdad on the banks of the river Tigris in the days of El-Ma'moun," she said with an emotion no less intense than mine.
>
> (trans. Denys Johnson-Davies, 1980, 142–3)

Abu Nuwas lived in Karkh, though shortly *before* "the days of El-Ma'moun". There seems little doubt, however, that Abu Nuwas holds together this passage in which he is both an object of academic fascination and, vicariously, through the imaginary presence of his persona, the facilitator of enchantment and infatuation. Mustafa Saʿeed is one of the more complex characters in Arabic literature. Brilliant in his studies in England, he becomes something of a polymath and utterly versed in English – not Arabic – literature. His attraction to Abu Nuwas, therefore, is superficially that of a wandering spirit to a literary icon of rebellion and libertinism.

At the end of the events of the novel Saʿeed returns home to Sudan but settles in a village that is foreign to him. It is hard to say that he is roundly tolerant at the end of his life (the novel avoids resolving matters in which there is inherent tension); but he does come to lie at the cusp of cultures yearning for some form of harmony. His mysterious library, hidden away in a recess of his house, proves the point strangely when it is unlocked after his disappearance. Having come to settle in the "South" he had secretly brought an extraordinary collection of books with him containing not a single Arabic volume (even the Qurʾan was in English). Abu Nuwas, who has something of the "universal figure" about him, might well have been one (if not the) point of cultural harmony for Saʿeed.

Iconoclasm and tolerant diversity exist side-by-side in Abu Nuwas, a poet who lies, chronologically and stylistically, at the very cusp of the most significant divisions in the classical tradition. He was immeasurably influential, for all that his unique legend of ribaldry tends to dominate the way he is remembered. And his importance in Arab literary history is perhaps commensurate with the fact that he is one of the most likeable of poets.

BIBLIOGRAPHY

ENGLISH TRANSLATIONS AND STUDIES

Drory, Rina. *Models and Contacts: Arabic Literature and Its Impact on Medieval Jewish Culture* (Boston: E.J. Brill, 2000), 48–59.

Gelder, Geert Jan van. "Dubious Genres: On Some Poems by Abū Nuwās". In *Arabica* 44 (1997), 268–83.

——. "Some Types of Ambiguity: A poem by Abū Nuwās on al-Faḍl al-Raqāshī". In *Quaderni di Studi Arabi*, 10 (1992), 75–92.

——. "Waspish Verses: Abū Nuwās's Lampoons on Zunbūr ibn Abī Ḥammād". In *Annali di Ca' Foscari*, 35 (1996), 447–55.

Hamori, Andras. *On the Art of Medieval Arabic Literature* (Princeton: Princeton University Press, 1973).

Ingrams, W.H. *Abu Nuwas in Life and Legend* (Mauritius: M. Gaud and Cie, 1933).

Kennedy, Philip F. *The Wine Song in Classical Arabic Poetry* (New York: Oxford University Press, 1997).

——. "Abū Nuwās, Samuel and Levi". In *Medieval and Modern Perspectives on Muslim-Jewish Relations*, 2 (1995), 109–25.

Lyons, Malcolm. *Identity and Identification in Classical Arabic Poetry* (Warminster: E.J.W. Gibb Memorial Trust, 1999).

Meisami, Julie. "Abū Nuwās and the Rhetoric of Parody". In *Festschrift Ewald Wagner zum 65. Geburtstag*, Wolfhart Heinrichs and Gregor Scholer (eds), (Beirut, 1994), 246–5.

Motoyoshi, Akiko. "Reality and Reverie: Wine and Ekphrasis in the 'Abbāsid Poetry of Abū Nuwās and al-Buḥturī". In *Annals of Japan Association for Middle East Studies*, 14 (1999), 85–120.

Montgomery, James E. "Abū Nuwās The Alcoholic". In U. Vermeulen and D. De Smet (eds), *Philosophy and Arts in the Islamic World* (Leuven, 1998), 16–26.

——. "Revelry and Remorse: A Poem of Abū Nuwās". In *Journal of Arabic Literature*, 25.1 (1994).

Montgomery, James E. "For the Love of a Christian Boy: A Song by Abū Nuwās". In *Journal of Arabic Literature*, 27 (1996), 114–24.

Ormsby, Eric. "Questions for Stones: On Classical Arabic Poetry". In *Parnassus: Poetry in Review* (available on-line at http://www.parnassuspoetry.com/Ormsby.htm).

Rowson, Everett K. *Homosexuality in Traditional Islamic Culture* (Columbia University Press, forthcoming; esp. chapter 3, "Baghdad: A Literary Revolution").

Salih, Talib. Season of Migration to the North, trans. D. Johnson-Davies (London, 1969; reprint 1980), 142–3.

Schoeler, Gregor. "Iblīs [the Devil] in the Poems of Abū Nuwās". In Angelika Neuwirth *et al.* (eds), *Myths, Historical Archetypes and Symbolic Figures in Arabic Literature* (Beirut, 1999), 271–90.

Smith, Rex. "Hunting Poetry", article in *The Cambridge History of Arabic Literature: 'Abbasid Belles-Lettres*, Julia Ashtiany ed. (Cambridge: CUP, 1990).

IMPORTANT STUDIES

In Arabic

Al-Nuwayhī, Muḥammad. *Nafsiyyat Abī Nuwās* (2nd edn.; Beirut, 1970).

In German

Wagner, Ewald. *Abū Nuwās: Eine Studie zur arabischen Literatur der frühen 'Abbāsidenzeit* (Wiesbaden, 1965) – contains the most thorough bibliographic guide to medieval sources.

Sezgin, F. *Geschichte des arabischen Schrifttums*, vol. 2 (Leiden: Brill, 1975) art. "Abū Nuwās", is also bibliographically invaluable.

In French

Bencheikh, J. "Poésies bachiques d'Abū Nuwās: thèmes et person-nages". In *Bulletin des Etudes Orientales* 18 (1963–4), 7–84.

Monteil, Vincent, *Abū Nuwās: le vin, le vent, la vie* (Paris, 1979).

ARABIC PRINTED EDITIONS OF COLLECTED POETRY

Ahlwardt, W. (ed.) *Diwan des Abu Nowas nach der Wiener und der Berliner Hds ..., I. Die Weinlieder* (Greifswald, 1861).

Wagner, Ewald (ed.) *Dīwān Abī Nuwās al-Ḥasan ibn Hāni'*, vols. 1–3 and 5; vol. 4, ed. Gregor Schoeler, (Wiesbaden and Cairo, 1958; Wiesbaden and Beirut, 1972–1988; vol. 5 forthcoming; = critical edition based on Ḥamza al-Iṣfahānī's [d. 971] redaction).

Al- Ḥadīthī, B. 'A. (ed.) *Dīwān Abī Nuwās* (Baghdad, 1980; = edition based on al-Ṣūlī's [d. c. 946] redaction, ∴ contains approx. a third of Ḥamza's lengthier redaction).

Al-Ghazālī, A. 'Abd al-Majīd (ed.) *Dīwān Abī Nuwās* (Cairo, 1953: has been widely used for reference until recently).

There are several other uncritical editions of which that of Īliyā Ḥāwī (Beirut: Dār al-Kitāb al-Lubnānī, 2 vols, 1987) is useful insofar as the poems are ordered alphabetically according to rhyme letter and can facilitate easy access to the full poems of individual verses cited in sundry medieval sources.

The *mujūn* (dissolute) category of poetry has been accessible in *Abū Nuwās: al-Nuṣūṣ al-Muḥarrama* [*The Forbidden Poems*], ed. Jamāl Jum'a (London: Saqi Books, 1994): = recent edition of *al-Fukāha wa-Itinās fī Mujūn Abī Nuwās*, Cairo 1898.

GENERAL READING AND REFERENCE

Robert Irwin's *Night and Horses and the Desert* (New York: Random House 2000) is a good starting point for further reading in classical Arabic literature generally, with a helpful bibliography.

The Encyclopedia of Arabic Literature, ed. J.S. Meisami and P. Starkey (London and New York: Routledge, 1998; 2 vols).

INDEX

Aban ibn 'Abd al-Hamid al-Lahiqi 10,
    101; satirical poem about 98–100
al 'Abbas ibn 'Abdallah, poetry in
    praise of 89–91
al-'Abbas ibn al-Ahnaf 12, 30
al-'Abbas ibn Musa al-Hadi 119
Abbasid poetry 32, 62
Abbasid society 18, 24
Abu 'Ali al-Hasan ibn Hani' al-Hakami
    see Abu Nuwas
Abu al-'Atahiya 12, 123, 125, 126
Abu Hilal al-'Askari 126
Abu al-Hindi 60
Abu Mihjan al-Thaqafi 26, 58, 59
Abu al-Najm al-'Ijli 110
Abu Nuwas: background 1–3;
    character and temperament 19–23;
    death 26–7, 106–7; education
    3–7; posthumous status 27–8,
    135–8; sexuality 16–19
Abu Tammam 81
Abu 'Ubayda Ma'mar ibn al-Muthanna
    6, 95
'Ad 50
'Adi ibn Zayd 123
Ahwaz 1, 3
al-Akhtal 95
'Ala' ibn al-Waddah 105–6
alchemy 102
'Ali ibn Abi Talib 98
al-A'ma al-Tutili 136
allusion 5, 18, 31, 46, 54, 56, 71, 75,
    77, 120
amatory prelude (nasib) 80–1, 83, 90
ambiguity 14, 32
al-Amin, Caliph 10, 18, 19; and
    hunting 109; imprisonment of Abu
    Nuwas 23, 24; lampoon of 97–8;
    poems written for 11, 92, 129, 130
'Amr al-Warraq 20
amrad 16

Ansari tribe 80
antithesis 14, 49, 77
Arabia, Northern and Southern tribes
    2, 90, 96
Arabian Nights 24, 27
Arabic poetry viii, ix, 3, 23, 73, 80,
    135; traditions of love poetry
    30–2; wine in 57–8
ascetic poetry 21, 73–4, 121–9
al-A'sha 14; Mu'allaqa 62–3
Ashja' al-Sulami 102
al-Asma'i 6
al-'Attabi, Kulthum ibn 'Amr 88
Ayyam al-'Arab 95

badi' x, 14, 15
Badr al-Juhani al-Barra' 17
Baghdad 90; Abu Nuwas' move to
    9–13; caliphate court 9, 10; poets
    in 10, 12
Bakr ibn al-Mu'tamir 97
Banawasi, Abu Nuwas known as 27
Banu 'Udhra 30
Barmecide family 9–11, 22, 25, 82,
    83, 101; elegies for 130–1
Barsum 106
Bashshar ibn Burd 31
Basra 1, 3, 7
al-Batin Sa'id ibn al-Walid 25
Bencheikh, J. 58–9
biblical references in poems 75, 77
boys 4; Christian 54–6; poems
    about 16; sexual preference for
    16–18
al-Buhturi, Abu 'Ubayda al-Walid 81

Cairo 26
cheetahs, poems about 114–15
Christian boys 54–6
Christian scripture, knowledge of
    55–6

Christians, treatment of in poems 20, 55–6, 70
contradiction, in poetry 77, 91
cynegetic poems 110

Damascus 26
'The Days' (al-Ayyam) 128
debate literature 92
desert, in verse 39, 61, 81, 88
Devil 4, 43–7, 73
al-Dhahabi 7
Di'bil ibn 'Ali 101
Dryden, John 14
Durra 68

Egypt 25–6; return from 83
elegies 27, 121, 129–33; for self 133–4
epitaph 34
erotic themes viii, 14, 16, 29–56
eulogies 10, 27

al-Fadl ibn Abi Sahl 103
al-Fadl ibn Rabi'a 9–10, 11, 91, 93, 97, 102; and imprisonment of Abu Nuwas 24, 82; poem dedicated to 88
al-Fadl ibn Yahya al-Barmaki 10–11, 79, 82
fakhr 57
fiqh (jurisprudence), understanding of 5
forbearance 74, 120
frivolity, in love poetry 35–6
funerary laments 129

genealogy 102, 124–5
generosity 20
ghazal (see also love poetry) x, 29, 36, 57
al-Ghazali 71
ghulamiyyat (transvestites) 17–18, 47, 68

hadith: knowledge of 5–6; teaching 7
Hafiz 3
al-Hajjaj ibn Yusuf 40
Hakam 72
Hamori, A. 74
Hani' ibn 'Abd al-Awwal (father) 2
Harun al-Rashid, Caliph 11, 19, 24,

25, 30, 91; elegy for 130; imprisonment of Abu Nuwas 23, 96; poetry in praise of 82–8
Harut 77
Hasan of Basra 93–4
Hashim ibn Hudayj 104
Hassan ibn Thabit 2, 80; 'Hamziyya' 80
al-Haytham ibn 'Adi, lampoon of 102
hedonism 58, 61, 64, 74
heresy 21, 100; imprisonment for 23
hija' (see also satire) x, 94, 95, 99, 106
Hims 25–6
Hira 27
homoerotic poems 18, 27, 32, 39
homosexuality 4, 18–19
hounds, elegy for 116–17
Humayd ibn Thawr 59
hunting poems viii, 87–8, 109–17
'Husayn', demon muse of Abu Nuwas 135–6
al-Husayn ibn al-Dahhak 12

ibahi 30, 31
Iblis see Devil
Ibn Butlan 104
Ibn al-Mu'tazz 5, 20
Ibn Nubata 111
Ibn Shuhayd, Epistle of Familiar Spirits 135–6
Ibn Zaydun 136
iltifat 38
imagining death 122
impotence, fear of 48–50
imprisonment 23–5
Imru' al-Qays 2, 6, 31, 60, 111
'Inan 105, 106; relationship with 37
Ingrams, W.H. 27
irreverence 22–3
'Isabadh 119
al-Isfahani 18, 19, 39, 40, 114, 117
Islam 74; influence of, in love poetry 30–1, 33
Isma'il ibn Abi Sahl, lampoon of 102–3, 107
Isma'il ibn Sabih 11

Jabriyya 21
Ja'far ibn Yahya 101, 102
Jahiliyya 57, 74

al-Jahiz 7, 18, 19, 92; *Book of Animals* 114; *Book of Misers* 96–7
Janan 3, 7–9, 105, 106; poems about 8
Jarada 7
Jarir 95
Jarrah ibn 'Abdullah al-Hakami 2
Jesus 99n
Jews, treatment of in verse 20, 70
Jonah 77
Jonson, Ben 64
Judgment (day) 123, 124, 128
Jullaban (mother) 1–2

Ka'b ibn Zuhayr 80
Karkh 13n, 137
Keats, John ix
Khalaf al-Ahmar, influence on Abu Nuwas 4–5, 6
khamriyyat (*see also* wine poetry) viii, x, 12, 74
al-Khansa' 129
al-Khasib 26, 81
Khurasan 18, 24
Khuzistan 1
Kufa 5; dissolutes of 36–7, 58, 100
kunya 69–70

Labid ibn Rabi 'a, *Mu 'allaqa* 88, 90
Lamiyyat al 'Arab 5
letters 52–4
love poetry 29–30; idealized love 32–5; and lust 35–7; master-servant relationships in 37–43; of seduction and rape 50–1; two traditions of 30–2
lust 35–7

madih (*see also* panegyric poetry) x, 121
Majnun Layla 70
al-Ma'mun, Caliph 19, 24, 97
Manhuka (poem by Abu Nuwas) 88
al-Mankli, Muhammad ibn 115
al-Mansur, Abu Ja'far, Caliph 89, 90
marriage of Abu Nuwas 16
marthiya (*see also* elegies) x
Marvel, Andrew ix
Marwan II, Caliph 2
Masarjasaya monastery 55

'Masjidites' 9
master-servant relationships, in love poetry 37–43
Mecca, pilgrimages to 8–9, 55, 89
metaphor 15, 116, 123, 124
Mirbad 13n
Modern poet, Abu Nuwas as 5, 6, 13–15
Monteil, V. 99n
Montgomery, J.E. 56
mu'allaqa x
mu'annathat 32
al-Mubarrad 83
mudhakkarat 18, 27, 32, 39
Muhammad the Prophet 80
muhdath x, 5, 6, 13–15
mujun x, 21, 37, 99, 128
munazara 92
Muslim, Abu Nuwas a 20
Muslim ibn al-Walid 12
al-Mu'tamid ibn 'Abbad 136
al-Mutanabbi 74, 95, 129
al-Mutawakkil, caliph 19
Mu'tazilism 22, 68

Nabat 106
naqa'id x, 95, 96
nasib (*see also* amatory prelude) x, 57, 64, 68, 72, 80–1
Al Nawbakht family 11, 12, 83; and death of Abu Nuwas 26, 27, 106–7
Nawruz 3
al-Nazzam, Ibrahim 22, 68

onomatopoeia 39
oryx tableau 87, 88

panegyric poetry 11, 79–81; for al-'Abbas ibn 'Abdallah 89–92; for al-Amin 11, 92; for Harun al-Rashid 82–8
paradox 33, 57, 75
parallelism 15, 16
paronomasia 15
Pasolini, Pier Paolo 27
patronage 9–12
patrons, poetry in praise of *see* panegyric poetry
Persian origins 1, 2–3
Persian vocabulary, use of 3, 26

polo match, poem about 117–20
posthumous status of Abu Nuwas
    27–8, 135–8
pre-Islamic poetry 5, 40, 80, 92, 122,
    123; love poems 31, 32, 34
prison, poems written in 82, 93–4

Qadariyya 21
qasida x, 30, 57, 58, 61
Qatrabbul 13n
Qu'ran 54; knowledge of 3, 6; use of
    vocabulary of 20, 26, 70–1, 120

rahil 81
rajaz 110
Ramadan 22
al-Raqashi 114
al-Rashid *see* Harun al-Rashid
religious tolerance 20–1
remuneration 79, 83
repentance 73, 74, 75
The Rescue of Hafs's Pupil (poem by
    Abu Nuwas) 42–3
rhetoric and rhetorical devices viii, x,
    14, 59, 65, 67, 80, 95, 122, 128
Rochester, John Wilmot, Earl of viii,
    107
Ronsard, Pierre de ix
Rowson, E.K. 16, 17

al-Sabbah (grandfather) 2
Sa'd ibn 'Ashira 2
Salih, Tayeb, *Season of Migration to the
    North* 136–8
saluki hounds, poems about 111–13
Saqr ibn Malik 119
satanic poems 43–7
satire 10, 22, 27, 37, 94–6, 106–7;
    on Aban 10, 98–9; and al-Amin
    97–8; of Barmecides 101–2; sexual
    103–5; of singing girls 105–6
sea, imagery of feminine sexuality 16,
    47
seduction, love poems about 50–1
sexual lampoons 103–5
sexuality of Abu Nuwas 16–19
al-Shafi'i 7
al-Shanfara al-Azdi 5
shatir 17
simplicity of language 125–6

singing girls, satire of 105–6
Skelton, John ix
Smith, R. 116–17
al-Suli 32, 39, 44, 128

tahlil 33
tardiyya (*see also* hunting poems) x,
    110, 111
tawba (repentance) 73, 74, 75
Tayf al-Khayal 34
theology, knowledge of 21–2
time 14, 64–5, 128
transvestites 17–18, 47, 68

'*udhri* 30–1, 33, 60–1
'Umar ibn Abi Rabi'a 30, 31, 59
Umayyad poetry 95, 110, 129
Umayyad society 2, 18
urjuza 110

Wagner, M. 115
al-Wahhab ibn 'Abd al-Majid
    al-Thaqafi 7
Waliba ibn al-Hubab 5, 27–8; elegy
    for 131–2; tutor of Abu Nuwas
    3–4, 27–8, 37, 64, 100
Walid ibn Yazid 60
wine 22, 137; in Arabic poetry 57–9;
    in panegyrics 83, 84
wine poetry viii, 13–15, 66–8;
    Baghdad and 12–13; *Dialogue with a
    Jewish Taverner* 68–71; and erotic
    themes 59–64; and repentance
    73–7; and time 64–5
women, poems about 16, 47–8
writing 52–4

Ya'qub ibn Ishaq al-Hadrami 6
Yusuf ibn Daya 23
Yusuf ibn Muhammad 98

Zakariya' al-Qushari 20
zandaqa 21
Zanzibar 27
Zubayda 18
Zuhayr ibn Musayyab 119
zuhdiyya (*see also* ascetic poetry) x,
    121, 125–6
'Zunbur' 94, 105, 106–7
zunnar 69

MAKERS *of the* MUSLIM WORLD

Series Editor: Patricia Crone
Institute for Advanced Study, Princeton

Among the over fifty titles in the series:

Ibn 'Arabi
William C. Chittick
Renowned expert William Chittick
surveys the life and works of this
legendary thinker.
ISBN: 1-85168-387-9

Shaykh Mufid
T. Bayhom-Daou
An assessment of the great Shi'ite
scholar and theologian.
ISBN: 1-85168-383-6

Abu Nuwas
Philip Kennedy
A readable introduction to this
celebrated 9th-century poet.
ISBN: 1-85168-360-7

'Abd al-Malik
Chase F. Robinson
The Umayyad Caliph and founder
of the Dome of the Rock is
captured in a concise and
clear manner.
ISBN: 1-85168-361-5

Fazlallah Astarabadi
and the Hurufis
Shahzad Bashir
Discusses the achievements of this
Sufi thinker and founder of Gnostic
Hurufism.
ISBN: 1-85168-385-2

al-Ma'mun
Michael Cooperson
An introduction to the controversial
9th-century Caliph and patron of the
sciences.
ISBN: 1-85168-386-0

Ahmad Riza Khan
Usha Sanyal
On the founder of the 'Barelwi'
movement in India in the late
19th/early 20th centuries.
ISBN: 1-85168-359-3

Amir Khusraw
Sunil Sharma
Surveys the life and work of the 14th-
century Indian poet, courtier, musician,
and Sufi.
ISBN: 1-85168-362-3

'Abd al-Rahman III
Maribel Fierro
Introduces the founder of the great
Caliphate of Madinat al-Zahra at
Cordova.
ISBN: 1-85168-384-4

el-Hajj Beshir Agha
Jane Hathaway
An examination of the longest serving
Chief Harem Eunuch in the history of
the Ottoman Empire.
ISBN: 1-85168-390-9

www.oneworld-publications.com